MORE
POETIC GEMS

SELECTED FROM THE WORKS

OF

WILLIAM McGONAGALL

Poet and Tragedian

Died in Edinburgh 29th September, 1902

WITH

BIOGRAPHICAL SKETCH AND REMINISCENCES

BY THE AUTHOR

EDITED BY Dr. D. W. SMITH

DUNDEE.
DAVID WINTER & SON LTD.
15 SHORE TERRACE

LONDON:
GERALD DUCKWORTH & CO. LTD
3 HENRIETTA ST W.C.2

1972

CONTENTS

		PAGE
The Autobiography of Sir William Topaz McGonagall	.	5
The Destroying Angel or the Poet's Dream	. . .	35
Lines in Defence of the Stage	. . . .	38
Calamity in London	. . . . .	40
The Black Watch Memorial	. . . .	43
Lost on the Prairie	. . . . .	47
The Irish Convict's Return	. . . .	48
Little Jamie	. . . . .	50
An Address to the Rev. George Gilfillan	. . .	51
An Address to Shakespeare	. . . .	52
The Fair Maid of Perth's House	. . . .	53
The Queen's Jubilee Celebrations	. . .	54
An Ode to the Queen	. . . . .	58
The Death of the Queen	. . . .	59
A Humble Heroine	. . . . .	61
Nora, the Maid of Killarney	. . . .	64
Little Popeet—The Lost Child	. . . .	66
The Little Match Girl	. . . . .	68
A Tale of Elsinore	. . . . .	69
The Bonnie Sidlaw Hills	. . . . .	72
Bonnie Callander	. . . . .	73
Bonnie Kilmany	. . . . .	75
Bonnie Montrose	. . . . .	77
Beautiful Comrie	. . . . .	78
Beautiful North Berwick	. . . .	79
Beautiful Crieff	. . . . .	81
Beautiful Balmoral	. . . . .	84
Beautiful Village of Penicuik	. . . .	85
Beautiful Nairn	. . . . .	86
Beautiful Torquay	. . . . .	88
The Ancient Town of Leith	. . . .	90

The City of Perth 93
Bonnie Dundee in 1878 94
Loch Ness 95
A Descriptive Poem on the Silvery Tay . . . 96
The Den o' Fowlis 97
The Inauguration of the Hill o' Balgay . . . 99
The Bonnie Lass o' Dundee 101
The Bonnie Lass o' Ruily 103
Mary, The Maid o' the Tay 106
The Heatherblend Club Banquet 108
The Summary History of Sir William Wallace . . 110
Lines in Praise of Tommy Atkins 112
The Relief of Mafeking 113
The Battle of Glencoe 116
The Capture of Havana 118
The Battle of Waterloo 121
The Albion Battleship Calamity 126
An All Night Sea Fight 129
The Wreck of the Steamer "Stella" 132
The Wreck of the Steamer "Storm Queen" . . 135
The Wreck of the "Abercrombie Robinson" . . 138
The Loss of the "Victoria" 142
The Burning of the Ship "Kent" 144
The Wreck of the "Indian Chief" 148
Captain Teach *alias* "Black Beard" . . . 150
The Disastrous Fire at Scarborough 153
The Burial of Mr Gladstone 155
The Death of the Rev. Dr. Wilson 158
The Death of Captain Ward 161
McGonagall's Ode to the King 164
A Soldier's Reprieve 165
Richard Piggot, The Forger 167
The Troubles of Matthew Mahoney 170

THE AUTOBIOGRAPHY

OF

SIR WILLIAM TOPAZ M'GONAGALL

POET AND TRAGEDIAN

Knight of the White Elephant, Burmah

My Dear Readers of this autobiography, which I am the author of, I beg leave to inform you that I was born in Edinburgh. My parents were born in Ireland, and my father was a handloom weaver, and he learned me the handloom weaving while in Dundee, and I followed it for many years, until it began to fail owing to machinery doing the weaving instead of the handloom. So much so as I couldn't make a living from it. But I may say Dame Fortune has been very kind to me by endowing me with the genius of poetry. I remember how I felt when I received the spirit of poetry. It was in the year of 1877, and in the month of June, when trees and flowers were in full bloom. Well, it being the holiday week in Dundee, I was sitting in my back room in Paton's Lane, Dundee, lamenting to myself because I couldn't get to the Highlands on holiday to see the beautiful scenery, when all of a sudden my body got inflamed, and instantly I was seized with a strong desire to write poetry, so strong, in fact, that in imagination I thought I heard a voice crying in my ears—

" WRITE! WRITE! "

I wondered what could be the matter with me, and I began to walk backwards and forwards in a great fit of excitement, saying to myself—" I know nothing about poetry." But still the voice kept ringing in my ears—" Write, write," until at last, being overcome with a desire to write poetry, I found paper, pen, and ink, and in a state of frenzy, sat me down to think what would be my first subject for a poem. All at once I thought of the late Rev. George Gilfillan, and composed a poem of four stanzas in his praise as a preacher, and orator, and poet. Then I sent it to the " Weekly News " for publication, not sending my name with it, only my initials—W. M'G., Dundee. It was published, along with a short comment by the editor in its praise, as follows :—" W. M'G., Dundee, has sent us a poem in praise of the Rev. George Gilfillan, and he sung his praises truly and well, but he modestly seeks to hide his light under a bushel," so when I read the poem in the " Weekly News " I was highly pleased no doubt to see such a favourable comment regarding it. Then my next poem, or second, was the " Railway Bridge of the Silvery Tay," which caused a great sensation in Dundee and far away. In fact, gentle readers, it was the only poem that made me famous universally. The reading of the poem abroad caused the Emperor of Brazil to leave his home far away incognito and view the bridge as he passed along *en route* to Inverness. But, my dear readers, the Tay Bridge poem is out of print, and I do not intend to publish it again, owing to the fall of the bridge in the year of 1879, which will be remembered for a very long time.

I may also state in this short autobiography of mine that my parents are dead some years ago—I don't remember how many, but they are buried in the Eastern Necropolis, Dundee, and I may say they were always good to me.

And now concerning something more attractive, my dear readers, I must inform ye that as early as ten years of age I was very fond of reading Shakespeare's Penny Plays (Vicker's edition), and from them I received great knowledge regarding the histrionic art. The plays or tragedies I studied most were Macbeth, Hamlet, Richard III, and Othello, the Moor of Venice, and these four characters I have impersonated in my time. During my stay in Dundee my

FIRST APPEARANCE ON THE STAGE

was in the character of Macbeth in Mr Giles' Penny Theatre, Lindsay Street, Dundee, to an overflowing and crowded audience, and I received unbounded applause. I was called before the curtain several times during the performance, and I remember the actors of the company felt very jealous owing to me getting the general applause, and several were as bold as tell me so ; and when it came to the combat scene betwixt me and Macduff the actor who was playing Macduff against my Macbeth tried to spoil me in the combat by telling me to cut it short, so as the audience, in his opinion, would say it was a poor combat, but I was too cute for him, guessing his motive for it. I continued the combat until he was fairly exhausted, and until there was one old gentleman in the audience cried out, " Well done, M'Gonagall! Walk into him!" And so I did until he was in a great rage, and stamped his foot, and cried out, " Fool! Why don't you fall ? " And when I did fall the cry was " M'Gonagall! M'Gonagall! Bring him out! Bring him out!" until I had to come before the curtain and receive an ovation from the audience. Such was the case in my second appearance, under the management of Forrest Knowles in the Grocers' Hall, Castle Street, Dundee. The characters I appeared in under his management were Macbeth, Richard III, and Hamlet. These three characters I performed to crowded and delighted audiences. I remember Mr Knowles told me in the dressing-room that I looked the character so well in the dress that I should wear it, and not throw it off, but I told him it was too great a joke to say so. I also remember on that night there were several gentlemen in the audience who were from Edinburgh, and they came to my dressing-room to congratulate me on my great success, and shook hands with me, telling me that few professionals could do it so well ; but perhaps they were only flattering me. If so, I will say with the poet, John Dryden—

> Flattery, like ice, our footing does betray,
> Who can tread sure on the smooth slippery way ?
> Pleased with the fancy, we glide swiftly on,
> And see the dangers which we cannot shun.

6

My dear readers, the next strange adventure in my life was my

JOURNEY TO BALMORAL

to see the bonnie Highland flora and Her Gracious Majesty the Queen, who was living in Balmoral Castle, near by the River Dee. Well, I left Dundee in the month of June, 1878. I remember it was a beautiful sunshiny day, which made my heart feel light and gay, and I tramped to Alyth that day, and of course I felt very tired and footsore owing to the intense heat. The first thing I thought about was to secure lodgings for the night, which I secured very easily without any trouble, and then I went and bought some groceries for my supper and breakfast, such as tea, sugar, butter, and bread. Then I prepared my supper, and ate heartily, for I had not tasted food of any kind since I had left Dundee, and the distance I had travelled was fifteen miles, and with the fresh air I had inhaled by the way it gave me a keen appetite, and caused me to relish my supper, and feel content. Then the landlady of the house, being a kind-hearted woman, gave me some hot water to wash my feet, as she thought it would make my feet feel more comfortable, and cause me to sleep more sound. And after I had gone to bed I slept as sound as if I'd been dead, and arose in the morning quite refreshed and vigorous after the sound sleep I had got. Then I washed my hands and face, and prepared my breakfast, and made myself ready for the road again, with some biscuits in my pocket and a pennyworth of cheese. I left Alyth about ten o'clock in the morning, and crossed over a dreary moor, stunted and barren in its aspect, which was a few miles in length—I know not how many—but I remember there were only two houses to be met with all the way, which caused me to feel rather discontented indeed. The melancholy screams of the peesweeps overhead were rather discordant sounds ringing in my ears, and, worst of all, the rain began to fall heavily, and in a short time I felt wet to the skin; and the lightning began to flash and the thunder to roar. Yet I trudged on manfully, not the least daunted, for I remembered of saying to my friends in Dundee I would pass through fire and water rather than turn tail, and make my purpose good, as I had resolved to see Her Majesty at Balmoral. I remember by the roadside there was a big rock, and behind it I took shelter from the rain a few moments, and partook of my bread and cheese, while the rain kept pouring down in torrents. After I had taken my luncheon I rose to my feet, determined to push on in spite of rain and thunder, which made me wonder, because by this time I was about to enter

> On the Spittal of Glenshee,
> Which is most dismal for to see,
> With its bleak and rugged mountains,
> And clear, crystal, spouting fountains
> With their misty foam ;
> And thousands of sheep there together doth roam,
> Browsing on the barren pasture most gloomy to see.
> Stunted in heather, and scarcely a tree,
> Which is enough to make the traveller weep,
> The loneliness thereof and the bleating of the sheep.

However, I travelled on while the rain came pouring down copiously and I began to feel very tired, and longed for rest, for by this time I had travelled about thirteen miles, and the road on

THE SPITTAL OF GLENSHEE

I remember was very stony in some parts. I resolved to call at the first house I saw by the way and ask lodgings for the night. Well, the first house chanced to be a shepherd's, and I called at the door and gently knocked, and my knock was answered by the mistress of the house. When she saw me she asked me what I wanted, and I told her I wanted a night's lodging and how I was wet to the skin. Then she bade me come inside and sit down by the fireside and dry my claes, and tak' aff my shoon and warm my feet at the fire, and I did so. Then I told her I came from Dundee, and that I was going to Balmoral to see Her Majesty the Queen, and that I was a poet. When I said I was a poet her manner changed altogether, and she asked me if I would take some porridge if she made some, and I said I would and feel very thankful for them. So in a short time the porridge were made, and as quickly partaken, and in a short time the shepherd came in with his two collie dogs, and the mistress told him I was a traveller from Dundee and a poet. When he heard I was a poet he asked me my name, and I told him I was M'Gonagall, the poet. He seemed o'erjoyed when he heard me say so, and told me I was welcome as a lodger for the night, and to make myself at home, and that he had heard often about me. I chanced to have a few copies of a twopence edition of poems with me from Dundee and I gave him a copy, and he seemed to be highly pleased with reading the poems during the evening, especially the one about the late George Gilfillan, and for the benefit of my readers I will insert it as follows. I may also state this is the first poem I composed, when I received the gift of poetry, which appeared in the " Weekly News " :—

LINES IN PRAISE OF THE REV. GEORGE GILFILLAN

All hail to the Rev. George Gilfillan, of Dundee,
He is the greatest preacher I did ever hear or see.
He preaches in a plain, straightforward way,
The people flock to hear him night and day,
And hundreds from his church doors are often
    turned away,
Because he is the greatest preacher of the present
    day.
The first time I heard him speak 'twas in the
    Kinnaird Hall,
Lecturing on the Garabaldi movement as loud as
    he could bawl.
He is a charitable gentlemen to the poor while in
    distress,
And for his kindness unto them the Lord will
    surely bless.
My blessing on his noble form and on his lofty head.
May all good angels guard him while living and
    hereafter when dead.

8

Well, my dear readers, after the shepherd and me had a social confab together concerning Gilfillan and poetry for some time his wife came in, and she said, " Guidman, I've been out making a bed for you in the barn. But maybe ye'll be feared tae sleep in the barn." But I said, " Oh, no, my good woman, not in the least." So she told her husband to show me the way to the barn, and he said, " Oh, yes, I'll do that, and feel highly honoured in doing so." Accordingly he got a lantern and lighted it, and then said—" Come along with me, sir, and I'll show you where to sleep for the night." Then he led the way to the barn, and when he entered he showed me the bed, and I can assure you it was a bed suitable for either King or Queen.

And the blankets and sheets
Were white and clean,
And most beautiful to be seen,
And I'm sure would have pleased Lord Aberdeen.

Then the shepherd told me I could bar the barn door if I liked if I was afraid to sleep without it being barred, and I said I would bar the door, considering it much safer to do so. Then he bade me good-night, hoping I would sleep well and come in to breakfast in the morning.

A STRANGE DREAM

After the shepherd had bidden me good-night I barred the door, and went to bed, as I expected to sleep ; but for a long time I couldn't—until at last I was in the arms of Morpheus, dreaming I was travelling betwixt a range of mountains, and seemingly to be very misty, especially the mountain tops. Then I thought I saw a carriage and four horses, and seemingly two drivers, and also a lady in the carriage, who I thought would be the Queen. Then the carriage vanished all of a sudden, and I thought I had arrived at Balmoral Castle, and in front of the Castle I saw a big Newfoundland dog, and he kept barking loudly and angry at me But I wasn't the least afraid of him, and as I advanced towards the front door of the Castle he sprang at me, and seized my right hand, and bit it severely, until it bled profusely. I seemed to feel it painful, and when I awoke, my dear readers, I was shaking with fear, and considered it to be a warning or a bad omen to me on my journey to Balmoral. But, said I to myself—

" Hence babbling dreams!
You threaten me in vain."

Then I tried hard to sleep, but couldn't. So the night stole tediously away, and morning came at last, peeping through the chinks of the barn door. So I arose, and donned my clothes, then went into the shepherd's house, but the shepherd wasn't in. He'd been away two hours ago, the mistress said, to look after the sheep on the rugged mountains. " But sit ye down, guidman," said she, " and I'll mak' some porridge for ye before ye tak' the road, for it's a dreary road to Balmoral." So I thanked her and husband for their kindness towards me, and telling her to give my best wishes to her husband bade her good-bye and left the shepherd's house for the Queen's Castle.

9

It was about ten o'clock in the morning when I left the shepherd's house at the Spittal of Glenshee on my journey to Balmoral. I expected to be there about three o'clock in the afternoon. Well, I travelled on courageously, and, when Balmoral Castle hove in sight, I saw the Union Jack unfurled to the breeze. Well, I arrived at the Castle just as the tower clock was chiming the hour of three. But my heart wasn't full of glee, because I had a presentiment that I wouldn't succeed. When I arrived at the lodge gate, I knocked loudly at the door of the lodge, and it was answered by a big, burly-looking man, dressed in a suit of pilot cloth. He boldly asked me what I wanted and where I had come from. I told him I had travelled all the way from Dundee expecting to see Her Majesty, and to be permitted to give an entertainment before her in the Castle from my own works and from the works of Shakespeare. Further, I informed him that I was the Poet M'Gonagall, and how I had been patronised by Her Majesty. I showed him Her Majesty's letter of patronage, which he read, and said it was a forgery. I said, if he thought so, he could have me arrested. He said this thinking to frighten me, but, when he saw he couldn't, he asked me if I would give him a recital in front of the Lodge as a specimen of my abilities. " No, sir," I said ; " nothing so low in my line of business. I am

NOT A STROLLING MOUNTEBANK

that would do the like in the open air for a few coppers. Take me into one of the rooms in the Lodge, and pay me for it, and I will give you a recital, and upon no consideration will I consent to do it in the open air."

Just at that time there was a young lady concealed behind the Lodge door hearkening all the time unknown to me. The man said, " Will you not oblige the young lady here ? " And when I saw the lady I said, " No, sir. Nor if Her Majesty would request me to do it in the open air, I wouldn't yield to her request." Then he said, " So I see, but I must tell you that nobody can see Her Majesty without an introductory letter from some nobleman to certify that they are safe to be ushered into Her Majesty's presence, and remember, if ever you come here again, you are liable to be arrested." So I bade him good-bye, and came away without dismay, and crossed o'er a little iron bridge there which spans the River Dee, which is magnificent to see. I went in quest of lodgings for the night, and, as I looked towards the west, I saw a farmhouse to the right of me, about half a mile from the highway. To it I went straightaway, and knocked at the door gently, and a voice from within cried softly, " Come in." When I entered an old man and woman were sitting by the fireside, and the man bade me sit down. I said I was very thankful for the seat, because I was tired and footsore, and required lodging for the night, and that I had been at Balmoral Castle expecting to see Her Majesty, and had been denied the liberty of seeing her by the constable at the Lodge gate. When I told him I had travelled all the way on foot from Dundee, he told me very feelingly he would allow me to stay with him for two or three days, and I could go to the roadside, where Her Majesty passed almost every day, and he was sure she would speak to me, as she always spoke to the gipsies and gave them money. The old woman, who was sitting in the corner at her tea, said, " Ay, and mind ye, guidman, it's no silver she gives them, it's gold. I'm sure Her Majesty's a richt guid lady. Mind ye, this is the Queen's bread I'm eating. Guidman, the mair, I canna see you. I'm blind, born blind, and I maun tell ye, as you're a poet, as I heard ye say, the Queen alloos a' the auld wimmen in the district here a loaf of bread, tea, and sugar, and a' the cold meat that's no used at the Castle, and, mind ye, ilka ane o' them gets an equal share." I said it was very kind of Her Majesty to do so, and she said, " That's no' a', guidman. She aye finds wark for idle men when she comes here— wark that's no needed, no' for hersel, athegether, but just to help needy folk, and I'm sure if you see her she will help you." So I thanked her for the information I had got, and then was conducted to my bed in the barn—a very good one—after I had got a good supper of porridge and milk. Then I went to bed,

NOT TO SLEEP, BUT TO THINK

of the treatment I had met with from the constable at the lodge of Balmoral Castle. I may state also that I showed the constable at the lodge a copy of my poems—twopence edition—I had with me, and he asked me the price of it, and I said, " Twopence, please." Then he chanced to notice on the front of it, " Poet to Her Majesty," and he got into a rage and said, " You're not poet to Her Majesty." Then I said, " You cannot deny that I am patronised by Her Majesty." Then he said, " Ah, but you must know Lord Tennyson is the real poet to Her Majesty. However, I'll buy this copy of your poems." But, as I said before, when I went to bed it was to think, not to sleep, and I thought in particular what the constable told me—if ever I chanced to come the way again I would be arrested, and the thought thereof caused an undefinable fear to creep all over my body. I actually shook with fear, which I considered to be a warning not to attempt the like again. So I resolved that in the morning I would go home again the way I came. All night through I tossed and turned from one side to another, thinking to sleep, but to court it was all in vain, and as soon as daylight dawned I arose and made ready to take the road. Then I went to the door of the farmhouse and knocked, and it was answered by the farmer, and he said, " 'Odsake, guidman, hoo have ye risen sae early ? It's no' five o'clock yet. Gae awa' back to your bed and sleep twa or three hours yet, and ye will hae plenty o' time after that tae gang tae the roadside to see Her Majesty." But I told him I had given up all thought of it, that I was afraid the constable at the lodge would be on the lookout for me, and if he saw me loitering about the roadside he would arrest me and swear falsely against me. Then he said, " Guidman, perhaps it's the safest way no' to gang, but, however, you'll need some breakfast afore ye tak' the road, sae come in by and sit doon there." Then he asked me if I could sup brose, and I said I could, and be thankful for the like. Then he cried, " Hi! lassie, come here and bile the kettle quick and mak' some brose for this guidman before he gangs awa'." Then the lassie came ben. She might have been about sixteen or seventeen years old, and in a short time she had the kettle boiling, and prepared for me a cog of brose and milk, which

11

I supped greedily and cheerfully, owing no doubt to the pure Highland air I had inhaled, which gave me a keen appetite. Then the farmer came ben and bade me good-bye, and told me to be sure and call again if ever I came the way, and how I would be sure to get a night's lodging or two or three if I liked to stay. So I bade him good-bye and the lassie and the old blind woman, thanking them for their kindness towards me. But the farmer said to the lassie, " Mak' up a piece bread and cheese for him for fear he'll no' get muckle meat on the Spittal o' Glenshee." So when I got the piece of bread and cheese again I bade them good-bye, and took the road for Glenshee, bound for Dundee, while the sun shone out bright and clear, which did my spirits cheer. After I had travelled about six miles, my feet got very hot, and in a very short time both were severely blistered. So I sat me down to rest me for a while, and while I rested I ate of my piece bread and cheese, which, I'm sure, did me please, and gave me fresh strength and enabled me to resume my travel again. I travelled on another six miles until I arrived at a lodging-house by the roadside, called

THE MILLER'S LODGING-HOUSE

because he had been a meal miller at one time. There I got a bed for the night, and paid threepence for it, and I can assure ye it was a very comfortable one ; and the mistress of the house made some porridge for me by my own request, and gave me some milk, for which she charged me twopence. When I had taken my porridge, she gave me some hot water in a little tub to wash my feet, because they were blistered, and felt very sore. And when my feet were washed I went to my bed, and in a short time I was sound asleep. About eight o'clock the next morning I awoke quite refreshed, because I had slept well during the night, owing to the goodness of the bed and me being so much fatigued with travelling. Then I chanced to have a little tea and sugar in my pocket that I had bought in Alyth, so I asked the landlady if she could give me a teapot, as I had some tea with me in my pocket, and I would infuse it for my breakfast, as I hadn't got much tea since I had left Dundee. So she gave me a teapot, and I infused the tea, and drank it cheerfully, and ate the remainder of my cheese and bread. I remember it was a lovely sunshiny morning when I bade my host and hostess good-bye, and left, resolved to travel to Blairgowrie, and lodge there for the night. So I travelled on the best way I could. My feet felt very sore, but

> As I chanced to see trouts louping in the River o'
> Glenshee,
> It helped to fill my heart with glee,
> And to anglers I would say without any doubt
> There's plenty of trouts there for pulling out.

When I saw them louping and heard the birds singing o'erhead it really seemed to give me pleasure, and to feel more contented than I would have been otherwise. At Blairgowrie I arrived about seven o'clock at night, and went in quest of a lodging-house, and found one easy enough, and for my bed I paid fourpence in advance. And when I had secured my bed I went out to try to sell a few copies of my poems. I had with me from Dundee the twopence edition, and I managed to sell half a dozen of copies with a great struggle. However, I was very thankful, because it would tide me over until I would arrive in Dundee. So with the shilling I had earned from my poems I bought some grocery goods, and prepared my supper—tea, of course, and bread and butter. Then I had my feet washed, and went to bed, and slept as sound as if I'd been dead. In the morning I arose about seven o'clock, and prepared my breakfast—tea again, and bread and butter. Then after my breakfast I washed my hands and face, and started for Dundee at a rapid pace, and thought it no disgrace. Still the weather kept good, and the sun shone bright and clear, which did my spirits cheer, and weary and footsore I trudged along, singing a verse of a hymn, not a song, as follows :—

> Our poverty and trials here
> Will only make us richer there,
> When we arrive at home, &c., &c.

When at the ten milestone from Dundee I sat down and rested for a while, and partook of a piece bread and butter. I toiled on manfully, and arrived in Dundee about eight o'clock, unexpectedly to my friends and acquaintances. So this, my dear friends, ends my famous journey to Balmoral. Next morning I had a newspaper reporter wanting the particulars regarding my journey to Balmoral, and in my simplicity of heart I gave him all the information regarding it, and when it was published in the papers it

CAUSED A GREAT SENSATION.

In fact, it was the only thing that made me famous—it and the Tay Bridge poem. I was only one week in Dundee after coming from Balmoral when I sent a twopence edition of my poems to the late Rev. George Gilfillan, who was on a holiday tour at Stonehaven at the time for the good of his health. He immediately sent me a reply, as follows :—

"Stonehaven, June, 1878.

" Dear Sir,—I thank you for your poems, especially the kind lines addressed to myself. I have read of your famous journey to Balmoral, for which I hope you are none the worse. I am here on holiday, but return in a few days.—Believe me, yours truly,

" GEORGE GILFILLAN."

Well, the next stirring event in my life which I consider worth narrating happened this way. Being out one day at the little village of Fowlis, about six miles from Dundee, and being in rather poor circumstances, I thought of trying to get a schoolroom to give an entertainment. But when I applied for the schoolroom I met with a refusal. Therefore, not to be beat, I resolved to try to get the smithy, and was fortunate in getting it. Then I went all over the village, or amongst the people, inviting them to my entertainment, chiefly from my own works and from Shakespeare. The prices were to be—Adults 2d., boys and girls 1d.,

13

and the performance was to commence at eight o'clock precisely. Well, when I had made it known amongst the villagers, some of them promised to come—chiefly ploughmen and some of the scholars. To while away the time, I called at the smith's house. The family had just sat down to supper, and the smith bade me draw in a chair to the table and take some supper, which consisted of tea and plenty of oaten cakes and loaf bread; also ham, cheese, and butter. So of course I drew in by my chair to the table, and fared very sumptuously, because I had got no refreshment since the morning before leaving Dundee. After supper, the smith said he would gang doon to the smithy wi' me, and gie it a bit redd up and get the lamp lighted.

THE SMITHY ENTERTAINMENT.

In a short time a few ploughmen came, and of course I was at the door to take the money, and they asked me the charge of admission, and I said—" Twopence, please." Then a few more people came—old and young—and they all seemed to be quite happy in expectation of the coming entertainment. When it was near eight o'clock the smith told me I would need to make ready to begin, so I told him to take the money at the door, and I would begin. He said he would do that cheerfully, and he took his stand at the door, and I addressed the audience as follows :—" Ladies and gentlemen, with your permission, I will now make a begnning by reciting my famous poem, ' Bruce at Bannockburn.' " Before it wias half finished I received great applause ; and when finished they were all delighted. Then followed " The Battle of Tel-El-Kebir " and a scene from " Macbeth " ; also " The Rattling Boy from Dublin," which concluded the evening's entertainment. The proceeds taken at the door amounted to 4s. 9d., and of course I was well pleased with what I had realised, because it is a very poor locality in that part of the country. Well, I thanked the audience for their patronage ; also the smith for allowing me the use of his smithy, and, bidding him good-night, I came way resolving to travel home again straightway. Well, as I drew near to Fowlis Schoolroom I heard the pattering of feet behind me and the sound of men's voices. So I was instantly seized with an indefinable fear, and I grasped my stick firmly in my right hand, and stood stock still, resolved to wait until the party behind would come up, and stood right in front of me, and neither of us spoke, when the centre man of the three whispered something to the two men that was with him, and then he threw out both arms, with the intention, no doubt, as I thought, of pulling my hat down over my eyes ; but no sooner were his arms thrown out than my good oaken cudgel came across his body with full force.

My Dear Friends,—I cannot describe to you my feelings at that moment. The cold sweat started to my forehead, but I was resolved to strike out in self-defence. Well, when I brought my good oaken cudgel over the ringleader's body he sprang back, and whispered to his companions, and they were forced to retire. As they were going the same road home as I was going, I thought it advisable not to go, so I took a back road, which leads up to the village of Birkhill, five miles from Dundee, and when I arrived at the village it was past eleven o'clock at

14

night. I went direct to the constable's house and rapped at the door, and it was answered by himself demanding who was there. I said, "A friend," so he opened the door, and he said—"Oh, it's you, Mr M'Gonagall. Come in. Well, sir, what do you want at this late hour?" "Well, sir," I said, "I've been down to-night giving an entertainment in the Smithy of Fowlis, and I've been attacked near to the Schoolroom of Fowlis by three men that followed me. One of the three, the centre one. threw out both of his arms, with the intention, no doubt, of pulling my hat down over my eyes; but this stick, sir, of mine, went whack against his body, which made him and his companions retire from the field. And now, as I am rather afraid to pass through Lord Duncan's woods, which are rather dreary and lonely, and the night being so dark, I want you sir, to escort me through the woods." Then he said he couldn't do that, looking to the lateness of the night, but, said he, "Just you go on, and if anyone offers to molest you, just shout as loud as you can, and I'll come to you." "But, my dear sir," I said, "three men could have me murdered before you could save me." "Well," he said, "I'll stand at the door for a little to see if anyone molests you, and I'll bid you good-night, Mr M'Gonagall, and safe home." I remember while passing through Lord Duncan's woods I recited to myself—

Yet though I walk through death's dark vale,
Yet will I fear none ill,
For Thou art with me, and Thy rod
And staff me comfort still.

Well, thank God, my dear friends, I arrived safe home to Dundee, shortly after twelve o'clock, and my family were very glad to see me safe home again, asking me why I had been so late in coming home. When I told them what I had been doing, giving an entertainment in the Smithy of Fowlis, and had been set upon by three men, they were astonished to hear it, and said that I should thank God that had saved me from being murdered. However, the four shillings and ninepence I fetched home with me—that I had gained from my entertainment—I gave all to my wife, and she was very thankful to get it, because the wolf was at the door, and it had come very opportune. Well, after I had warmed myself at the fire, and taken a cup of tea, and bread and butter, I went to bed, but didn't sleep very sound. I suppose that was owing to the three men that attacked me in the home-coming. Well, my dear readers, the next stirring event that I will relate is

MY TRIP TO AMERICA.

In my remembrance, that is about fourteen years ago, and on the 9th of March I left Dundee. But before I left it I went amongst all my best friends and bade them good-bye, but one particular good friend I must mention, the late Mr Alexander C. Lamb, proprietor of the Temperance Hotel, Dundee. Well, when I called to bid him good-bye, and after we had shaken hands warmly, he asked me if any of my pretended friends had promised to take me home again from America if I failed in my enterprise. So I told him not one amongst them had promised. "Well," says he, "write to me and I will fetch you home."

Then on the next day, after bidding good-bye to my friends and relations in Dundee, I left Dundee with the train bound for Glasgow, and arrived safe about four o'clock in the afternoon. When I arrived I went to a good temperance hotel, near to the Broomielaw Bridge, and secured lodgings for the night, and before going to bed I prepared my supper—tea, of course, and bread and butter—and made a good meal of it. Then I went to bed, but I didn't sleep very sound, because my mind was too much absorbed regarding the perilous adventure I was about to undertake. Well, at an early hour the next morning I got up and washed myself, and prepared my breakfast, and made ready to embark on board the good steamship " Circassia," bound for the city of New York. When I went on board all was confusion, and there was a continuous babel of voices amongst the passengers, each one running hither and thither in search of a berth. And I can assure ye, my friends, it was with a great deal of trouble I secured a berth, because there were so many passengers on board. Well, when all the passengers had got their berths secured for the voyage, and the anchor had been weighed, and the sails hoisted, the big steamer left the Clyde with upwards of 500 souls, bound for New York. Some of them were crying, and some were singing, and some were dancing to the stirring strains of the pibroch. Such is life I say, throughout the world every day, and it was on the 10th of March we sailed away bound for America. As the stout steamer entered the waters of the Atlantic Ocean some snow began to fall, and a piercing gale of wind sprang up, but the snow soon ceased, and the wind ceased also, and the vessel sped on rapidly through the beautiful blue sea, while the cooks on board were preparing the passengers' tea. Yes, my dear readers, that's the supper the passengers get every night—plenty of bread, butter, and tea ; and coffee, bread, and butter for breakfast ; and for dinner, broth or soup and bread and beef. This is the fare in general going and coming. Well, when a week at sea all of a sudden the vessel began to roll, and the sea got into a billowy swell. The vessel began to heave fearfully, and the big waves began to lash her sides and sweep across her deck, so that all the boxes and chests on deck and below had to be firmly secured to prevent them from getting tossed about, and to prevent them from making a roaring sound like thunder. Many of the passengers felt seasick, and were vomiting, but I didn't feel sick at all. Well, the next day was a beautiful sunny day, and all the passengers felt gay, and after tea was over it was proposed amongst a few of them to get up

A CONCERT ON BOARD

that night. I was invited by a few gentlemen, and selected as one of the performers for the evening, and was told to dress in Highland costume, and that I would receive a collection for the recitations I gave them. The concert was to begin at eight o'clock. Well, I consented to take part in the concert, and got a gentleman to dress me, and when dressed I went to the second cabin, where the concert was to be held, and when I entered the cabin saloon I received a hearty round of applause from the passengers gathered there. Among them were the chief steward of the vessel. He

was elected as chairman for the evening, and addressed us as follows :—
" Ladies and gentlemen,—I wish it to be understood that all collections
of money taken on board this vessel at concerts go for the benefit of the
Lifeboat Fund, and I also hope you will also enjoy yourselves in a decent
way, and get through with the concert about ten o'clock, say. As Mr
M'Gonagall, the great poet, is first on the programme, I will call on him
to recite his own poem ' Bruce at Bannockburn.' "

So I leapt to my feet and commenced, and before I was right begun
I received a storm of applause, but that was all I received for it. Well,
when I came to the thrusts and cuts with my sword my voice was drowned
with applause, and when I had finished I bade them all good-night, and
retired immediately to my berth in the steerage, and undressed myself
quickly, and went to bed, resolving in my mind not to dress again if I
was requested on the home-coming voyage. Well, my friends, the vessel
made the voyage to New York in twelve days—of course night included
as well—and when she arrived at the jetty or harbour of New York some
of the passengers, when they saw it, felt glad, and others felt sad,
especially those that had but little money with them. As for myself, I
had but eight shillings, which made me feel very downcast, because all
the passengers are examined at Castle Gardens by the officials there
regarding the money they have with them, and other properties. Well,
when I came to the little gate where all the passengers are questioned
regarding their trades and names before they are allowed to pass, and if
they want their British money changed for American money, I saw at
once how I could manage. So after the man had entered my name and
trade in his book as a weaver, I took from my purse the eight shillings,
and laid it down fearlessly, and said—" Change that! It is all I require
in the meantime." So the man looked at me dubiously, but I got passed
without any more trouble after receiving the American money. Then I
passed on quickly until I saw a car passing along the way I was going.
So I got into the car, and I asked the carman where was Forty-Nine
Street. He said he was just going along that way, and he would let me
off the car when he came to it. So he did, honestly. Then I went to an
old acquaintance of mine while in Dundee, and rang the door bell, and
it was answered by my friend. When he saw me he stood aghast in
amazement, but he bade me come in, and when I entered the house
his wife bade me sit down, and sit near to the fire, for nae doubt I would
feel cold after being on the sea sae lang. So the mistress said I'll mak' ye
a cup o' tea, for ye'll be hungry, nae doubt, and I said I was so. Tea was
prepared immediately, and my friend and his wife sat down at the table
together, and made a hearty meal, and seemingly they were very sociable
until we had finished eating, and the table removed. Then my friend
asked me why I had ventured to come to New York. So I told him it was
in expectation of getting engagements in music halls in the city, and he
said he was afraid I wouldn't succeed in getting an engagement. As he said
it came to pass, for when I went three days after being in New York to
look for engagements at the music halls I was told by all the managers
I saw that they couldn't give me an engagement, because there was a
c mbination on foot

and how I had come at a very bad time. When I couldn't get an engagement I thought I would try and sell some of my poems I had fetched with me from Dundee. Well, the first day I tried to sell them it was a complete failure for this reason—When they saw the Royal coat of arms on the top of the poems they got angry, and said, " To the deuce with that. We won't buy that here. You'll better go home again to Scotland." Well, of course, I felt a little angry, no doubt, and regretted very much that I had been so unlucky as to come to New York, and resolved in my mind to get home again as soon as possible. When I came back to my friend's house, or my lodging-house in New York, I told him how I had been treated when I offered my poems for sale, and he said to me, " I'll tell you what to do. You'll just cut off the Royal coat-of-arms, and then the people will buy them from you." And when he told me to do so I was astonished to hear him say so, and told him " No! " I said, " I decline to do so. I am not ashamed of the Royal coat-of-arms yet, and I think you ought to be ashamed for telling me so, but you may think as you like, I will still adhere to my colours wherever I go."

WEARYING FOR HOME.

Well, after I had been three weeks in New York without earning a cent I thought I would write home to Dundee to Mr Alexander C. Lamb, proprietor of the Temperance Hotel, Dundee. Well, I remember when writing to my dear friend, the late Mr Lamb, I told him for God's sake to take me home from out of this second Babylon, for I could get no one to help me, and when writing it the big tears were rolling down my cheeks, and at the end of the letter I told him to address it to the Anchor Line Steam Shipping Company's office, to lie till called for. So, when the letter was finished I went out to the Post Office and posted it. Well, to be brief, I remember the next day was Sunday, and in the evening of the same day my friend invited the most of his neighbours to his house, as there was going to be a concert held amongst them, and, of course, I was invited to the concert and expected to recite, of course. And after the neighbours had been all seated and ready to begin my friend was elected by the neighbours to occupy the chair for the evening, and he said, " Ladies and gentlemen,—As we are all assembled here to-night to enjoy ourselves in a sociable manner, it is expected that all those that can sing a song will do so, and those that can recite will do the same, and as my friend here, the great Poet, M'Gonagall, can recite, I request him to open the concert by reciting his own poem, ' Bruce at Bannockburn.' "

I leapt to my feet and said, " Mr Chairman, ladies and gentlemen,—I refuse to submit to such a request, because I believe in God, and He has told us to remember the Sabbath day to keep it holy, and I consider it is an act of desecration to hold a concert on the Sabbath. Therefore, I refuse to recite or sing."

" Oh, but," the Chairman said, " it is all right here in New York. mmoconœtiu here."

Then there chanced to be a Jew in the company, and he said to me, " What you know about God ? Did ever He pay your rint ? " And I said, " Perhaps He did. If He didn't come down from Heaven and pay it Himself, He put it in the minds of some other persons to do it for Him." Then the Jew said, " You'll petter go home again to Scotland. That won't do here." Then the lady of the house said—" If ye dinna recite to obleege the company ye'll juist need tae gang oot. Ye ought to be ashamed o' yersel, for look how ye have affronted me before my neighbours."

Then I said—" But I haven't affronted God." Then the Jew said— " What you know about God ? Did you ever see Him ? " " Not in this company at least," I replied. And then I arose and left the company, considering it to be very bad, and retired to my bed for the night, thinking before I fell asleep that I was in dangerous company, because, from my own experience, the people in New York in general have little or no respect for the Sabbath. The theatres are open, also the music halls, and all of them are well patronised. My dear readers, I will now insert in this autobiography of mine a poem, " Jottings of New York," which will give you a little information regarding the ongoings of the people, which runs as follows :—

DESCRIPTIVE POEM—JOTTINGS OF NEW YORK

Oh, mighty city of New York, you are wonderful to behold—
Your buildings are magnificent—the truth be it told—
They were the only thing that seemed to arrest my eye,
Because many of them are thirteen storeys high ;
And as for Central Park, it is lovely to be seen—
Especially in the summer season when its shrubberies are green
And the Burns Statue is there to be seen,
Surrounded by trees on the beautiful sward so green ;
Also Shakespeare and the immortal Sir Walter Scott,
Which by Scotchmen and Englishmen will never be forgot.

There are people on the Sabbath day in thousands resort—
All lov'd, in conversation, and eager for sport ;
And some of them viewing the wild beasts there,
While the joyous shouts of children does rend the air—
And also beautiful black swans, I do declare.

And there's beautiful boats to be seen there,
And joyous shouts of children does rend the air,
While the boats sail along with them o'er Lohengrin Lake,
And fare is 5 cents for children, and adults ten is all they take.

And there's also summer-house shades, and merry-go-rounds,
And with the merry laughter of the children the park resounds,
During the live-long Sabbath day,
Enjoying themselves at the merry-go-round play.

Then there's the elevated railroads about five storeys high,
Which the inhabitants can hear night and day passing by;
Of, such a mass of people there daily do throng—
No less than five 100,000 daily pass along;
And all along the city you can get for five cents—
And, believe me, among the passengers there's few discontent.

And the tops of the houses are mostly all flat,
And in the warm weather the people gather to chat;
Besides, on the housetops they dry their clothes;
And, also, many people all night on the housetops repose.

And numerous ships and steamboats are there to be seen,
Sailing along the East River water, which is very green—
Which is certainly a most beautiful sight
To see them sailing o'er the smooth water day and night.

And as for Brooklyn Bridge, it's a very great height,
And fills the stranger's heart with wonder at first sight;
And with all its loftiness I venture to say
It acnnot surpass the new railway bridge of the Silvery Tay.

And there's also ten thousand rumsellers there—
Oh, wonderful to think of, I do declare!
To accommodate the people of New York therein,
And to encourage them to commit all sorts of sin.

And on the Sabbath day ye will see many a man
Going for beer with a big tin can,
And seems proud to be seen carrying home the beer
To treat his neighbours and his family dear.

Then at night numbers of the people dance and sing,
Making the walls of their houses to ring
With their songs and dancing on Sabbath night,
Which I witnessed with disgust, and fled from the sight.

And with regard to New York and the sights I did see—
Believe me, I never saw such sights in Dundee;
And the morning I sailed from the city of New York
My heart it felt as light as a cork.

Well, my dear readers, to resume my autobiography, I've told ye I
sent a letter to Mr Alexander C. Lamb in Dundee requesting him to fetch
me to Dundee as he had promised, and when about three weeks had
expired I called at the Anchor Line Steam Shipping Company's office on
a Monday morning, I remember, to see if a letter had come from Dundee.
Well, when I asked Mr Stewart if there was any news from Dundee, he
said, " Yes," smiling at me, and, continuing—" Yes, I received a cable-
gram from Dundee on Saturday night telling me to give you a passage

home again—a second class cabin, not the steerage this time." And he asked me how much money I would require, and I told him about three pounds. "But," he said, " I've been told to give you six," and when he told me so I felt overjoyed, and thanked him and my dear friend, Mr Alexander C. Lamb. Then he asked me if I would take British money or American, and I said I would take American one half and British the other, and along with it he gave me a certificate for my passage on board the " Circassia," which would sail from New York harbour in about a fortnight or so, telling me to be sure and not forget the time the steamer would leave New York for Glasgow, and bidding me to be watchful regarding my money, for there were many bad characters in New York.

Well, my dear friends, I bade him good-bye, telling him I would take his good advice, and, if alive and well, I would be on the lookout for the steamer that was to take me to Bonnie Scotland, and left him with my heart full of glee.

Well, my dear friends, at last the longed-for day arrived that I was to leave New York, and everything I required being ready, I bade farewell to my old Dundee friend and his mistress, and made my way down to the jetty or harbour of New York, where the beautiful steamer "Circassia" lay that I was to embark in, which would carry me safe to Glasgow and the rest of the passengers, God willing. And when I arrived at the jetty there were a great number of intending passengers gathered ready to go on board, and there was a great deal of hand-shaking amongst them, bidding each other good-bye. Some of them were crying bitterly, noticed, and others were seemingly quite happy. Such is life.

> Some do weep, and some feel gay,
> Thus runs the world away.

Well, when the hand-shakings were over, the intending passengers went on board, and I amongst the rest. The first thing that arrested my attention was the skirling of the pibroch, playing

" WILL YE NO COME BACK AGAIN ? "

and other old familiar Scottish airs, and the babbling of voices, mingling together with rather discordant music ringing in my ears. The sails were hoisted, and steam got up, and the anchor was weighed, and the bell was rung. Then the vessel steamed out of New York Harbour, bound for Glasgow. The stout vessel sailed o'er the mighty deep, and the passengers felt delighted, especially when an iceberg was sighted. I remember I saw two large ones while going to America. Now, on the return voyage one has been sighted, and a very big one, about ten feet high, which in the distance has a very ghostly appearance, standing there so white, which seemed most fearful to the passengers' sight. And some of the passengers were afraid that it might come towards the vessel, but it remained immovable, which the passengers and captain were very thankful for. Well, on sped the vessel for a week without anything dangerous happening until the sea began all of a sudden to swell, and the waves rose up like mountains high ; then the vessel began to roll from side to side in the trough of the sea, and the women began to scream and the children also.

21

The big waves swept o'er her deck, so much so that the hatches had to be nailed down, and we all expected to be drowned in that mighty ocean of waters. Some parts, the steward told me, were five miles deep. When he told me so I said to him, " Is that a fact ? " and he said it was really true. And I said to him how wonderful it was and how beautiful and dark blue the sea was, and how I had often heard of

THE DARK BLUE SEA,

but now I was sailing o'er it at last. The vessel all at once gave a lurch and slackened her speed, and the cause thereof was owing to the piston of one of the engines breaking in the centre, which rendered it unworkable, and it couldn't be repaired until the vessel arrived in Glasgow. By that break in the engine we were delayed three days longer at sea, and, strange to say, as I remarked to some of the passengers, " Isn't it wonderful to think that the sea calmed down all at once as soon as the piston broke ? " And some said it was and others said it wasn't, and I said in my opinion it was God that calmed the sea—that it was a Providential interference, for, if the sea hadn't calmed down, the vessel would have been useless amongst the big waves owing to the engine giving way, and would have sunk with us all to the bottom of the briny deep, and not one of us would have been saved. Well, my friends, after that I was looked upon as a prophet and a God-fearing man, and very much respected by the passengers and the chief steward. So on the next evening there was to be a concert held amongst the passengers, and they all felt happy that they were spared from a watery grave, and many of them thanked God for saving them from being drowned. So the next day the sea was as calm as a mirror, and the vessel skimmed o'er the smooth waters like a bird on the wing, and the passengers felt so delighted that some of them began to sing. When evening set in, and the passengers had got their tea, arrangements were made to hold the concert in the cabin saloon, as formerly, and, of course, I was invited, as before, to give my services. This is generally expected on board of all emigrant vessels. Any one known to be a singer or a reciter will join in the entertainment for the evening, because emigrants either going or returning from a foreign country are all like one family. There seems to be a brotherly and a sisterly feeling amongst them, more so at sea than on land. No doubt the reason is that they are more afraid of losing their lives at sea than on land.

A CONCERT AT SEA.

When it drew nigh to eight o'clock all those who intended to be present at the concert began to assemble in the cabin saloon, and by eight o'clock the saloon was well filled with a very select gathering of passengers. Of course, amongst them was the chief steward and myself as formerly. Of course he was elected as chairman, and as formerly he announced that all collections of money on board at concerts went for the benefit of the Lifeboat Fund. Now there was amongst the passengers an actor, who had been to New York in expectation of getting engagements there, and had failed, and was well known to the chief steward, and had consented

22

to give a recital along with a lady from the play of " The Lady of Lyons." She was to read her part from the book, and he was to recite his part from memory, he taking the part of Claude Mellnotte, and she " the Lady of Lyons." So such being the case the audience thought they were going to get a treat, so the chairman announced them as first on the programme to give a recital, which was received with applause when announced. But that was all the applause they received during their recital, for she stammered all along in the reading of her part, and as for the actor he wasn't much better. All the difference was he remembered his part, but his voice was bad. Then when they had finished their recital I was requested to give a recital, and I recited Othello's Apology, which was received with great applause. Then I was encored, and for an encore I sang " The Rattling Boy from Dublin," and received thunders of applause. When I had finished several of the passengers shook hands with me warmly, telling me I had done well. Then other songs followed from ladies and gentlemen. And the chairman sang a song, and we all felt quite jolly, and free from melancholy, while the vessel sped on steadily as a rock. By this time it was near ten o'clock, and as it was near time to finish up with the concert, I was requested by the chairman to give another recital, which would conclude the evening's entertainment. So I consented, and recited " The Battle of Tel-el-Kebir," and received the general applause of the audience. This finished the evening's entertainment. Then there was shaking of hands amongst the passengers, and high compliments were paid to those that joined in the concert, myself included. So we all retired to rest, highly pleased with the evening's entertainment, and I slept fairly well that night. In the morning I was awakened from my sleep by someone knocking at the door of my berth, gently, and I asked who was there. A voice replied, " A friend." I arose at once to see who had knocked, and there was one of the gentlemen who had heard me recite at the concert, and he asked me if I was open to receive from him a few shillings as

A TOKEN OF REWARD,

and his appreciation of my abilities as a reciter, telling me he considered it a great shame for passengers to allow me to give them so much for nothing. So I thanked him for his kindness, and he said—" Don't mention it," and bade me good morning, saying he was going to have breakfast, and that he would see me again. So in a short time the bell rang for breakfast, and I was served, as well as others, with a small loaf of bread and butter and a large tin of hot coffee, which in general is the morning fare—quite enough, in my opinion, for any ordinary man. Well, my friends, I have nothing more of any importance to relate concerning my return from New York, any more than that we arrived safe and well at Glasgow, after being fourteen days at sea on the home-coming voyage. The next morning I took an early train bound for Dundee, and arrived there shortly after one o'clock noon. When I arrived at home my family were very glad to see me ; and also some of my old friends ; and as I had written a diary regarding my trip to New York I sold it to a newspaper reporter, who gave me 7s. 6d. for it.

FAREWELL TO DUNDEE.

Well, my dear friends, the next event in my life that I am going to relate is regarding me and my Mistress M'Gonagall leaving Dundee in the year 1894, resolving to return no more owing to the harsh treatment I had received in the city, as is well known for a truth without me recording it. Well, I went to the Fair City of Perth, one of the finest upon the earth, intending to remain there altogether. So I secured a small garret in the South Street, and me and my mistress lived there for eight months, and the inhabitants were very kind to us in many respects. But I remember receiving a letter from an Inverness gentleman requesting me to come through on the 16th October and give him and his friends an entertainment, and that all arrangements had been made with the directors of the Inverness Railway Company, and that I had only to show the letter. Well, I went down to the Railway Station and showed the officials the letter from Inverness inviting me through, and when they read it they said it was all right. They had received a telegram regarding it, and they told me to come down in the morning a little before ten o'clock, so as I could leave Perth with the ten o'clock train, and they would give me a certificate that would make me all right for the return journey to Perth. So I thanked them, telling them I would be down in the morning, God willing, in good time. When I went home I told my wife that I had made all right for my railway trip to Inverness, and she was glad to hear that it was all right. When I had got my supper I went to bed, but I didn't sleep well, for I was thinking too much about venturing so far away entirely amongst strangers, but as I had been assured of

A HEARTY HIGHLAND WELCOME.

I considered I was safe in making the venture. So I screwed up my courage and all danger regarding my trip to Inverness vanished from my mind. In the morning I arose and donned my clothes, and partook of a hearty meal along with my good lady, and then made myself ready for going to Inverness. When ready I bade my mistress good-bye, and away I went to the railway station and saw the officials. When the train for Inverness was nearly ready to start they showed me into one of the carriages, and bade me good-bye.

The train steamed off with its long white curling cloud of steam which was most beautiful to be seen. The train passed rocky mountains and woodland scenery, and lochs and rivers, and clear crystal fountains gushing from the mountains, and the bleak, heathery hills made the scenery very romantic to the appearance I remember. But it was only a bird's eye view I had, the train passed on so quickly, but in the summer season I thought it would be delightful to be roaming at ease, and to be viewing the mountain scenery and the beautiful villas by the way near to the riverside, surrounded by trees and shrubberies. As for the angler, he could have excellent sport fishing in the lochs and the river in that Highland region near to Dalwhinnie and other beautiful places I noticed by the way. And while thinking so in my mind I was astonished to think that the train had arrived, before I knew, and there I was met at the station by the gentleman who had written to me. He asked me if I was the Poet M'Gonagall, and I said I was, and he grasped me by the hand kindly, and told me to follow him. I did so without fear, and he took me to a hotel. And as we entered it we were met by the landlord, to whom I was introduced. And the proprietor told me there and then not to be ashamed to ask for anything I liked that was in the house, and I would get it, because the gentleman that had fetched me through from Perth had told him so, and with that my friend left me to my own meditations. Then I told the hotel proprietor I would have for dinner some coffee, bread, and a beefsteak, so in a very short space of time my dinner was ready and served out to me by a servant girl, and I did ample justice to it because I felt hungry. By this time it was about five o'clock in the afternoon, so I went out to have a walk and view the beautiful scenery along the riverside, and after I did so it was within an hour for me to entertain the gentleman who had brought me from Perth, so I had some tea made ready, and ate heartily, and when finished my friend came in and asked me if I had been enjoying myself, and I told him I had. Then he said the gentlemen I was to entertain would soon drop in. So they began to drop in by twos and threes until the room was well filled. The large table in the room was well spread with costly viands. When we had all partaken of the good spread on the table a chairman was elected, a gentleman of the name of Mr Gossip, and a very nice gentleman he was. He began by saying—" Gentlemen! I feel proud to-night to be elected at this meeting of friends and acquaintances to hear the great poet, Mr M'Gonagall, displaying his poetic abilities from his own works and from other poets also, and I request, gentlemen, that we will give him patient hearing, and I am sure if ye do ye will get a poetic treat, for his name is a household word at the present day. Therefore, gentlemen, with these few remarks I will call upon our distinguished guest, Mr M'Gonagall, to favour the company with a recital of his famous poem, ' Bannockburn.' "

I arose and said—" Gentlemen, I feel proud to-night to be amongst such a select company of gentlemen, and as far as my abilities will permit me I'll endeavour to please ye, and by your kind permission I will now begin to recite my Bannockburn poem."

Before I was halfway through, the cheering from the company was really deafening to my ears, so much so that I had to halt until the cheering subsided, and when I finished the company shook hands with me all round. After I sat down one of the gentlemen said he would sing a song on my behalf while I was resting, but he said he would need to get a glass of wine first. So when he got the glass of wine and drank to my health he began to sing that song of Burns', " Gae bring tae me a pint of wine." I can assure ye, my readers, he sang the song very well, and with so much vehemence that when he had finished

HE WAS FAIRLY EXHAUSTED,

and all for my sake. And when done his head fell upon his shoulder, and he seemed to be in the arms of Morpheus. Then other gentlemen sang songs, and the night passed by pleasantly, and all went well. Then the chairman said—" Gentlemen, as the night is far advanced I will now call upon our guest of the evening, Mr M'Gonagall, to give us a song— ' The Rattling Boy from Dublin,' of which he is the author."

Then I said—" Mr chairman and gentlemen, I am quite willing to do so, owing to the kind treatment I have met with, and the hearty Highland welcome ye have bestowed upon me, which I will not forget in a hurry. So I will begin to sing my song." Before I was halfway through, the gentleman who had fallen asleep in the chair awoke, and leapt on to the floor, and began to dance, until the chairman had to stop him from dancing, and when order was restored I went on with my song without any further interruption. And when I finished my song I recited " The Battle of Tel-el-Kebir," also a scene from Macbeth, which seemed to please the company very well. That was owing, I think, to Macbeth living in Inverness at one time.

Well, my dear friends, that concluded the evening's entertainment. Then the gentleman who had sent me the letter to come through to Inverness to give his friends an entertainment arose and said—" Mr chairman and friends,—It now falls to my lot to present to the great poet, M'Gonagall, this purse of silver, of which it is the desire of my friends and myself never to make known the contents. So saying, he handed me the purse and its contents, which I thanked him for and the company, telling them that I would never forget their kindness, and that in all my travels I had never met with such good treatment. Then the gentlemen all round shook hands with me, declaring they were well pleased with the entertainment I had given them. Wishing me good night and a sound sleep, they left me to my own meditations ; but my friend, before leaving me, conducted me to my bed in the hotel, and wishing me good-night, he said he would see me in the morning, and see me off in the train for Perth. So I went to bed, quite delighted with the treatment I had received from the gentlemen I had entertained in Inverness, and in the morning I was up with the lark, and had a good breakfast, and put a good luncheon piece in my pocket to eat by the way returning to Perth. My friend called on me in the morning, and accompanied me to the Railway Station, and saw me off by the ten o'clock train for Perth, and I arrived safe in Perth about half-past four o'clock on the afternoon of the 17th day of October, 1894.

Two days after my arrival from Inverness I composed a poem in praise of the Heather Blend Club banquet at Inverness, which is as follows :—

'Twas on the 16th of October, in the year 1894,
I was invited to Inverness, not far from the sea shore,
To partake of a banquet prepared by the Heather Blend Club,
Gentlemen who honoured me without any hubbub.

The banquet was held in the Gellion Hotel,
And the landlord, Mr Macpherson, treated me right well ;
Also the servant maids were very kind to me,
Especially the girl that polished my boots, most beautiful to see

26

The banquet consisted of roast beef, potatoes, and red wine:
Also hare soup and sherry and grapes most fine,
And baked pudding and apples lovely to be seen ;
Also rich sweet milk and delicious cream.

Mr Gossip, a noble Highlander, acted as chairman,
And when the banquet was finished the fun began ;
And I was requested to give a poetic entertainment,
Which I gave, and which pleased them to their hearts' content.

And for my entertainment they did me well reward
By titling me there the Heather Blend Club bard ;
Likewise I received an illuminated address,
Also a purse of silver, I honestly confess.

Oh, magnificent city of Inverness,
And your beautiful river, I must confess,
With its lovely scenery on each side,
Would be good for one's health there to reside.

There the blackbird and mavis together doth sing,
Making the woodlands with their echoes to ring
During the months of July, May, and June,
When the trees and the shrubberies are in full bloom.

And to see the River Ness rolling smoothly along,
Together with the blackbird's musical song,
While the sun shines bright in the month of May,
Will help to drive dull care away.

And Macbeth's Castle is grand to be seen,
Situated on Castle Hill, which is beautiful and green.
'Twas there Macbeth lived in days of old,
And a very great tyrant he was be it told.

I wish the members of the Heather Blend Club every success,
Hoping God will prosper them and bless ;
Long may Dame Fortune smile upon them,
For all of them I've met are kind gentlemen.

And in praise of them I must say
I never received better treatment in my day,
Than I received from my admirers in Bonnie Inverness.
This, upon my soul and conscience, I do confess.

My dear readers, I must now give you a brief account of my trip to
the mighty city of London. If I can remember, it might be either 19 or
20 years ago, and in the merry month of June, when trees and flowers
were in full bloom, and owing to my poverty I couldn't have gone to
London, only that I received a letter—a forged one—supposed to be

written by Dion Boucicault, the Irish dramatist, inviting me down to Stratton's Restaurant at twelve o'clock noon to have lunch with him, as he intended to engage me for a provincial tour to give entertainments in the provincial towns throughout Britain, and he would give me a big salary. Well, my dear friends, of course I felt delighted when I read the letter, so I went to Stratton's Restaurant just as the town clock struck twelve. I was received very kindly, and shown upstairs to a little room. I think it was the smoking room, and I knocked at the door, and it was answered by one of the gentlemen. Of course I knew him, and he introduced me to the gentleman who was impersonating the character of Dion Boucicault, and he asked me how I was, and I told him I was very well, hoping to find him the same. Then he told me he had heard so much about my histrionic abilities that he would engage me and give me a salary of £20 weekly, food included, and the other gentlemen present said it was little enough for a man of my abilities ; but all the while I knew he was an impostor. Then he requested me to recite my famous poem, " Bruce at Bannockburn," and of course I did so, and when finished he declared if I would recite that before a Scottish audience in London it would pull down the house. Then he told one of the gentlemen to fetch in some refreshment for Mr M'Gonagall, for he was more than delighted with my Bannockburn recital. Then a gentleman waiter came in with a little refreshment on a tea tray, simply

> A penny sandwich and a tumbler of beer,
> Thinking it would my spirits cheer.

And I remember I looked at it with a scornful eye before I took it, and I laid it down on a little round table beside me and screwed my courage to the sticking place, and stared the impostor Boucicault in the face, and he felt rather uneasy, like he guessed I knew he wasn't the original Boucicault, so he arose from his seat and made a quick retreat, and before leaving he bade me good-bye, telling me he would see me again. Then I kept silent, and I stared the rest of my pretended friends out of countenance until they couldn't endure the penetrating glance of my poetic eye, so they arose and left me alone in my glory. Then I partook of the grand penny luncheon I had received for my recital of " Bannockburn," and with indignation my heart did burn.

I went direct to the Theatre Royal, and inquired for Mr Hodge, the manager, and I saw him and I showed him the letter I had received from Dion Boucicault, as I didn't believe it was from him, and when he looked at it he said it wasn't his handwriting, and how I had met with a great disappointment no doubt, and asked me if I would allow him to make an extract from the letter and he would send it to Boucicault, so I said I would ; so he made an extract, telling me he mentioned my poor circumstances in it, and he had no doubt but Mr Boucicault would do something for me by way of solatium for my wounded feelings and for using his name in vain. He told me to come down to the theatre inside of three days, and he would have a letter from Boucicault by that time, he expected, so I thanked him for his kindness, and came away with my spirits light andgay.

Well, I waited patiently till the three days were expired, then called at the Theatre Royal and saw Mr Hodge, the manager, and he received me very kindly, telling me he had received a letter from Mr Boucicault with a £5 cheque in it on the Bank of Scotland, so he handed me five sovereigns in gold along with Boucicault's letter. I thanked him and came away, and in the letter Boucicault felt for me very much, saying practical jokers were practical fools, which in my opinion is really true. So, my dear readers, it was through me getting the £5 from Boucicault that I resolved to take a

TRIP TO LONDON.

A steerage return passage at that time was £1, so I purchased a ticket and made up my mind to go. I remember it was in the month of June, when trees and flowers were in full bloom, and on a Wednesday afternoon I embarked on board the steamer " London," and there were a few of my friends waiting patiently at the dockyard to see me off to London and wish me success in my perilous enterprise, and to give me a hearty cheer my spirits for to cheer, and a merry shake of hands all round, which made the dockyard loudly resound. Then when the handshakings were o'er the steam whistle began to roar. Then the engine started, and the steamer left the shore, while she sailed smoothly o'er the waters of the Tay, and the passengers' hearts felt light and gay. There weren't many passengers, I remember, but seemingly they all felt merry as the steamer drew near to Broughty Ferry, because the scenery in that direction is very fascinating to be seen, the seascape so lovely and green. When the steamer had passed by Broughty Ferry a few miles I remember the passengers began to get weary, and we were all sitting on the deck, and some of them proposed that they should have a song, so a lady sang a song, but I don't remember the name of it ; it's so long ago, but it's of no great consequence. When they had all sung I was requested to give a recital, and I gave them the " Battle of Tel-el-Kebir," which was well received, and I got an encore, and I gave them the " Rattling Boy from Dublin Town," and for which I received a small donation, and that finished the entertainment for the night. Then the steerage passengers bade me good-night and retired to their berths for the night, and me along with the rest. Well, the steamer sailed smoothly along during the night, and nothing happened that would the most timid heart affright, and the passengers slept well, including myself, owing to the smooth sailing of the good ship.

All went smoothly as a marriage bell until the good steamer landed us safe at the wharf, London, in the River Thames. Then there was shaking of hands and bidding each other good-bye, and each one took their own way, some on holiday, others on the look-out for work ; such was the case with me. Well, as soon as I got ashore I held on by the Fish Market, and as I drew near very discordant sounds broke upon my ear. The babbling of the fishmongers was disagreeable to hear ; and I had my properties with me in a black bag, and as I was passing along where there were about thirty men lounging near to the market-place they cried after me, " Hi! hi! Scottie, I'll carry your bag," but I paid no heed to them, because I would never have seen it if I had allowed any-one of them to have carried the bag. However, I made my way to Fetter Lane, Fleet Street, and secured my lodgings for a week in the White Horse Inn, Fetter Lane, at 4d. per night, so for the time being I was all right.

I PAID THE LANDLORD IN ADVANCE

for my lodging, and had some supper, and then I gave him my bag to lock up; then my mind felt quite at ease. Then I went out to have a walk, and resolved to call at the Lyceum Theatre and see—now Sir— Henry Irving. He wasn't Sir Henry then, my friends. Well, I made straight for the theatre and saw the janitor at the stage entrance, and I asked him if I could see Mr Irving, and he said snappishly I could not, and that Mr Irving wouldn't speak to the likes of me. Well, of course, I felt indignant, and I told him I considered myself to be as great a man as he is, and came away without delay; but he will speak to me now, my friends, and has done so in Edinburgh. Well, after I had come home to my lodgings from the theatre I made my supper quickly, and relished it with a good appetite. I requested the landlord to show me to bed, and he did so cheerfully, and wished me good-night and sweet repose. Each lodger had an enclosed apartment to himself of wood and a door, which he can lock if he likes to do so. However, I went to bed and slept soundly during the night, and arose in the morning, when the sun was shining bright. Then I donned my clothes, and made my breakfast, and took it with great gusto; then, when finished, I went out and wended my way towards London Bridge, and, oh! such a busy throng of cabs and 'buses rapidly whirling along. After viewing it, I returned to my lodging quite delighted with the sight I had seen, and then I prepared my dinner a few hours afterwards, and ate heartily. Then I went to some of the Music Halls looking for engagements, but, unfortunately, I didn't succeed. Owing to the disappointments I met with, I resolved to return home to Dundee as soon as possible. Well, when Sabbath came round, I went to the Tabernacle to hear Mr Spurgeon preach, and I most solemnly declare he is the greatest preacher I've ever heard, with the exception of Gilfillan.

However, as I resolved to return home to Dundee, I waited for the day Saturday to come. That was the day the steamer " London " would leave London for Dundee, and when Saturday came I left my lodgings in Fetter Lane, longing, of course, for to get hame, and embarked on board, with my heart light, and longing to see the Silvery Tay. So the stout steamer from the Thames sailed away, and arrived on Wednesday in the Silvery Tay, and the passengers' hearts were full of glee when they were landed safely in Dundee once again. I was glad to see it, especially my family. In conclusion, I will insert my poem,

"JOTTINGS OF LONDON."

As I stood upon London Bridge,
And viewed the mighty throng
Of thousands of people in cabs and 'buses
Rapidly whirling along,
And driving to and fro,
Up one street and down another
As quick as they could go.

Then I was struck with the discordant sounds
Of human voices there,
Which seemed to me like wild geese
Cackling in the air.

And as for the River Thames—
It is a most wonderful sight ;
To see the steamers and barges
Sailing up and down upon it
From early morn till night.

And as for the Tower of London—
It is most gloomy to behold,
And within it lies the Crown of England
Begemmed with precious stones and gold.

Kingly Henry the Sixth was murdered there
By the Duke of Gloster,
And when he killed him with his sword
He called him an impostor.

St. Paul's Cathedral is the finest building
That ever I did see ;
There's nothing can surpass it
In the town of Dundee,
For it is most magnificent to behold
With its beautiful dome and lofty spire glittering like gold.

And as for Nelson's Monument
That stands in Trafalgar Square—
It is a most stately statue
I most solemnly declare,
And towering very high,
Which arrests strangers' attention
When they are passing by.
And there's two beautiful water fountains
Spouting up very high,
Where the weary travellers can have a drink
When they feel dry

31

Then at the foot of Nelson's Monument
There's three figures of bronze lions in grand array,
Which ought to drive dull care away
As the stranger gazes thereon,
Unless he is very woebegone.

Then as for Mr Spurgeon,
He is a divine surgeon,
Which no one can gainsay.
I went to hear him preach on the Sabbath day,
Which made my heart feel light and gay
For to hear him preach and pray.

And the Tabernacle was crowded from ceiling to floor,
And many people were standing outside the door.
He is an eloquent preacher, I solemnly declare,
And I was struck with admiration as I on him did stare ;
For he is the only individual I heard
Speaking proper English during my stay there.

Then as for Petticoat Lane, I venture to say
It's a most wonderful place to see on the Sabbath day ;
For wearing apparel of every kind
Can be bought to suit the young and the old
For the ready money—silver, copper, or gold.

My Dear Readers,—I must now tell ye my reason for leaving the
Fair City of Perth. It was because I found it to be too small for me
making a living in. I must allow, the inhabitants were very kind to me
during my stay mongst them. And while living there I received a letter,
and when I opened it I was struck with amazement when I found a
silver elephant enclosed, and I looked at it in amazement, and said—
" I'll now have a look at this big letter enclosed. I was astonished to see
that King Theebaw, of Burmah and the Andaman Islands, had conferred
upon me the honorary title of Sir Wm. Topaz M'Gonagall, Knight of The
White Elephant, Burmah, and for the benefit of my readers and the
public, I consider I am justified in recording it in my autobiography,
which runs as follows :—

                              Court of King Theebaw,
                                Andaman Islands,
                                  Dec. 2, 1894.

    Dear and Most Highly Honoured Sir,—Having the great honour to
belong to the same holy fraternity of poets as yourself, I have been
requested by our fellow-country-men at present serving our Queen and
country in Her Majesty's great Indian Empire to send you the following
address, and at the same time to inform you that you were lately ap-
pointed a Grand Knight of the Holy Order of the White Elephant,
Burmah, by his Royal Highness upon representation being made to him
by your fellow-countrymen out here

King Theebaw, who is just now holding his Court in the Andaman Islands, expressed himself as being only too pleased to confer the highest honour possible upon merit, wheresoever found, if that merit were judged worthy by his Grand Topaz General. As the latter gentleman has long been impressed by the injustice with which you have been treated by Lord Rosebery in his position as chief adviser of Her Majesty, and since your great modesty upon several occasions has been noticed by His Royal Highness the King of Burmah, it gives him great pleasure to assure Theebaw, the King, that none more worthy of this high honour has ever lived in the East, whereat His Royal Highness called his Court together, and with much eclat and esteem caused it to be proclaimed throughout his present palace and kingdom that you were to be known henceforth as Topaz M'Gonagall, G.K.H.O.W.E.B.

Should you ever visit the Andaman Islands it will be his great pleasure to be presented to you, and to do all honour to you, according to the very ancient custom with which members of our mutual illustrious Order have always been treated by his ancestors.

That you will consent to accept the high honour now offered to you is the wish nearest the hearts of your countrymen in the East ; that you may be long spared to enrich British literature by your grand and thrilling works is their most sincere prayer.

His Majesty also expressed it as his opinion, and the opinion of hie grandfathers as far back as the flood, that such talented works as thoss of their holy fraternity of poets were, had always been, and for ever would be, above all earthly praise, their value being inestimable. He further stated that he failed to conceive how Rosebery could have been so blind as not to have offered to such a man as yourself the paltry and mean stipend attached to the position of Poet Laureate of Great Britain and Ireland. It is indescribable to him that any man of ordinary rummel gumption could possibly offer remuneration to such a gift of the Gods as yours.

Should you see fit to do the ancient Kingdom of Burmah the honour of accepting the Ribbon of its highers Order, and will kindly pay its capital a visit at your earliest convenience, it is the King's order that you be received with all the ceremony due to the greatest ornament now living of the Holy Order of the White Elephant. You are to be immediately installed in the holy chair of the Knights of the above Order upon arrival, from which it is the custom of the holy fraternity to address the whole Eastern world.

King Theebaw will not injure your sensitive feelings by offering you any filthy lucre as payment for what you may compose in his honour after receiving the insignia of the Holy Order. He also states it will be his duty to see that your name is duly reverenced throughout the Kingdom.

I have the honour to be, most noble and illustrious sir, your most humble brother in the fraternity of poets.

(Per) C. MACDONALD, K.O.W.E.B.,

Poet Laureate of Burmah.

By order of His Royal Highness the King.

Topaz General.
Topaz Minister.
Secretary of State.
Holder of Seals.
Registrar-General.
Staff-Bearer.
Secretary of Letters Patent.
Keeper of the White Elephant.

My dear readers, this letter regarding my knighthood is a correc copy from the original as near as I can write it, with the exception of the Indian language therein, which means the names of the gentlemen that signed the Royal patent letter regarding my knighthood. That is all that is wanting, which I cannot write or imitate. Nor can I imitate the four red seals that are affixed to the Royal document. The insignia of the knighthood is a silver elephant attached to a green silk ribbon.

This, my dear readers, is the full particulars regarding my Indian knighthood, and, my dear friends and well-wishers, I must conclude this autobiography of mine by truthfully recording herein that since I came to beautiful Edinburgh, and that is more than six years now past, I have received the very best of treatment, and during my stay in Edinburgh I have given many entertainments from my own poetic works, also from Shakespeare.

I may say I have been highly appreciated by select audiences, and for their appreciation of my abilities I return them my sincere thanks for being so kind as to give me their support since I came to Edinburgh.—Mr dear friends, I am, yours faithfully,

SIR WM. TOPAZ M'GONAGALL,
Poet and Knight of the White Elephant,
Burmah.

McGONAGALL

THE DESTROYING ANGEL
OR THE POET'S DREAM

I dreamt a dream the other night
That an Angel appeared to me, clothed in white.
Oh! it was a beautiful sight,
Such as filled my heart with delight.

And in her hand she held a flaming brand,
Which she waved above her head most grand;
And on me she glared with love-beaming eyes,
Then she commanded me from my bed to arise.

And in a sweet voice she said, " You must follow me,
And in a short time you shall see
The destruction of all the public-houses in the city,
Which is, my friend, the God of Heaven's decree."

Then from my bed in fear I arose,
And quickly donned on my clothes;
And when that was done she said, " Follow me
Direct to the High Street, fearlessly."

So with the beautiful Angel away I did go,
And when we arrived at the High Street, Oh! what a show.
I suppose there were about five thousand men there,
All vowing vengeance against the publicans, I do declare.

Then the Angel cried with a solemn voice aloud
To that vast and Godly assembled crowd,
" Gentlemen belonging the fair City of Dundee,
Remember I have been sent here by God to warn ye.

35

" That by God's decree ye must take up arms and follow me
And wreck all the public-houses in this fair City,
Because God cannot countenance such dens of iniquity.
Therefore, friends of God, come, follow me.

" Because God has said there's no use preaching against
strong drink,
Therefore, by taking up arms against it, God does think,
That is the only and the effectual cure
To banish it from the land, He is quite sure.

" Besides, it has been denounced in Dundee for fifty years
By the friends of Temperance, while oft they have shed tears.
Therefore, God thinks there's no use denouncing it any
longer,
Because the more that's said against it seemingly it grows
stronger."

And while the Angel was thus addressing the people,
The Devil seemed to be standing on the Townhouse Steeple,
Foaming at the mouth with rage, and seemingly much
annoyed,
And kicking the Steeple because the public-houses were
going to be destroyed.

Then the Angel cried, " Satan, avaunt! begone! "
Then he vanished in the flame, to the amazement of every-
one ;
And waving aloft the flaming brand,
That she carried in her right hand

She cried, " Now, friends of the Temperance cause, follow
me :
For remember it's God's high decree

36

To destroy all the public-houses in this fair City;
Therefore, friends of God, let's commence this war immediately."

Then from the High Street we all did retire,
As the Angel, sent by God, did desire;
And along the Perth Road we all did go,
While the Angel set fire to the public-houses along that row.

And when the Perth Road public-houses were fired, she cried, " Follow me,
And next I'll fire the Hawkhill public-houses instantly."
Then away we went with the Angel, without dread or woe,
And she fired the Hawkhill public-houses as onward we did go.

Then she cried, " Let's on to the Scouringburn, in God's name."
And away to the Scouringburn we went, with our hearts aflame,
As the destroying Angel did command.
And when there she fired the public-houses, which looked very grand.

And when the public-houses there were blazing like a kiln,
She cried, " Now, my friends, we'll march to the Bonnet Hill,
And we'll fire the dens of iniquity without dismay,
Therefore let's march on, my friends, without delay."

And when we arrived at the Bonnet Hill,
The Angel fired the public-houses, as she did well.
Then she cried, " We'll leave them now to their fate,
And march on to the Murraygate."

Then we marched on to the Murraygate,
And the Angel fired the public-houses there, a most deserving
fate.
Then to the High Street we marched and fired them there,
Which was a most beautiful blaze, I do declare.

And on the High Street, old men and women were gathered
there,
And as the flames ascended upwards, in amazement they did
stare
When they saw the public-houses in a blaze,
But they clapped their hands with joy and to God gave
praise.

Then the Angel cried, " Thank God, Christ's Kingdom's near
at hand,
And there will soon be peace and plenty throughout the land,
And the ravages of the demon Drink no more will be seen."
But, alas, I started up in bed, and behold it was a dream!

LINES IN DEFENCE OF THE STAGE

Good people of high and low degree,
I pray ye all be advised by me,
And don't believe what the clergy doth say,
That by going to the theatre you will be led astray.

No, in the theatre we see vice punished and virtue rewarded,
The villain either hanged or shot, and his career retarded ;
Therefore the theatre is useful in every way,
And has no inducement to lead the people astray.

Because therein we see the end of the bad man,
Which must appal the audience—deny it who can—
Which will help to retard them from going astray,
While witnessing in a theatre a moral play.

The theatre ought to be encouraged in every respect,
Because example is better than precept,
And is bound to have a greater effect
On the minds of theatre-goers in every respect.

Sometimes in theatres, guilty creatures there have been
Struck to the soul by the cunning of the scene ;
By witnessing a play wherein murder is enacted,
They were proven to be murderers, they felt so distracted,

And left the theatre, they felt so much fear,
Such has been the case, so says Shakespeare.
And such is my opinion, I will venture to say,
That murderers will quake with fear on seeing murder in a
    play.

Hamlet discovered his father's murderer by a play
That he composed for the purpose, without dismay,
And the king, his uncle, couldn't endure to see that play,
And he withdrew from the scene without delay.

And by that play the murder was found out,
And clearly proven, without any doubt ;
Therefore, stage representation has a greater effect
On the minds of the people than religious precept.

We see in Shakespeare's tragedy of Othello, which is sub-
    lime,
Cassio losing his lieutenancy through drinking wine ;

And, in delirium and grief, he exclaims—
" Oh, that men should put an enemy in their mouths to steal
    away their brains! "

A young man in London went to the theatre one night
To see the play of George Barnwell, and he got a great fright;
He saw George Barnwell murder his uncle in the play,
And he had resolved to murder his uncle, but was stricken
    with dismay.

But when he saw George Barnwell was to be hung
The dread of murdering his uncle tenaciously to him clung,
That he couldn't murder and rob his uncle dear,
Because the play he saw enacted filled his heart with fear.

And, in conclusion, I will say without dismay,
Visit the theatre without delay,
Because the theatre is a school of morality,
And hasn't the least tendency to lead to prodigality.

CALAMITY IN LONDON

FAMILY OF TEN BURNED TO DEATH

'Twas in the year of 1897, and on the night of Christmas day,
That ten persons' lives were taken away,
By a destructive fire in London, at No. 9 Dixie Street,
Alas! so great was the fire, the victims couldn't retreat.

In Dixie Street, No. 9, it was occupied by two families,
Who were all quite happy, and sitting at their ease ;
One of these was a labourer, David Barber and his wife,
And a dear little child, he loved as his life.

40

Barber's mother and three sisters were living on the ground
     floor,
And in the upper two rooms lived a family who were very
     poor,
And all had retired to rest, on the night of Christmas day,
Never dreaming that by fire their lives would be taken away.

Barber got up on Sunday morning to prepare breakfast for
     his family,
And a most appalling sight he then did see ;
For he found the room was full of smoke,
So dense, indeed, that it nearly did him choke.

Then fearlessly to the room door he did creep,
And tried to arouse the inmates, who were asleep ;
And succeeded in getting his own family out into the street,
And to him the thought thereof was surely very sweet.

And by this time the heroic Barber's strength was failing,
And his efforts to warn the family upstairs were unavailing ;
And, before the alarm was given, the house was in flames,
Which prevented anything being done, after all his pains.

Oh! it was a horrible and heart-rending sight
To see the house in a blaze of lurid light,
And the roof fallen in, and the windows burnt out,
Alas! 'tis pitiful to relate, without any doubt.

Oh, Heaven! 'tis a dreadful calamity to narrate,
Because the victims have met with a cruel fate ;
Little did they think they were going to lose their lives by
     fire,
On that night when to their beds they did retire.

It was sometime before the gutted house could be entered in,
Then to search for the bodies the officers in charge did begin ;
And a horrifying spectacle met their gaze,
Which made them stand aghast in a fit of amaze.

Sometime before the Firemen arrived,
Ten persons of their lives had been deprived,
By the choking smoke, and merciless flame,
Which will long in the memory of their relatives remain.

Oh, Heaven! it was a frightful and pitiful sight to see
Seven bodies charred of the Jarvis' family ;
And Mrs Jarvis was found with her child, and both
    carbonised,
And as the searchers gazed thereon they were surprised.

And these were lying beside the fragments of the bed,
And in a chair the tenth victim was sitting dead ;
Oh, Horrible! Oh, Horrible! what a sight to behold,
The charred and burnt bodies of young and old.

Good people of high and low degree,
Oh! think of this sad catastrophe,
And pray to God to protect ye from fire,
Every night before to your beds ye retire.

THE BLACK WATCH MEMORIAL

Ye Sons of Mars, it gives me great content
To think there has been erected a handsome monument
In memory of the Black Watch, which is magnificent to see,
Where they first were embodied at Aberfeldy.

And as a Highland regiment they are worthy of what has
      been done for them,
Because a more courageous regiment we cannot find of men
Who have bravely fought and bled in defence of their
      country,
Especially in the Russian War and Soudan War they made
      their enemies flee.

The monument I hope will stand secure for many a long day,
And may the people of Aberfeldy always feel gay ;
As they gaze upon the beautiful Black Watch monument,
I hope they will think of the brave soldiers and feel content.

'Twas in the year of 1887, and on Saturday the 12th of
      November,
Which the people of Aberfeldy and elsewhere will remember,
Who came all the way from Edinburgh, Glasgow, Perth and
      Dundee,
Besides the Pitlochry Volunteers headed the procession right
      manfully.

And the Perthshire Rifles joined the procession with their
      pipe band,
Then followed a detachment of the 42nd Highlanders so
      grand,

Under the command of Lieutenant M'Leod,
Whose duty it was to represent the regiment of which he
     felt proud.

The pipe band of the Glasgow Highlanders also were there,
And Taymouth Brass Band, which discoursed sweet music
     I do declare ;
Also military officers and the magistrates of Aberfeldy,
While in the rear came the members of Committee.

There were also Freemasons, Foresters, all in a row,
And wearing their distinctive regalias, which made a great
     show ;
And the processionists were formed into three sides of a
     square
Around the monument, while the music of the bands did
     rend the air.

The noble Marquis of Breadalbane arrived on the ground at
     1.30,
Escorted by a guard of honour and his pipe band ;
Then the bands struck up, and the pipes were set a bumming,
And all with one accord played up the " Campbell's are
     Coming."

Then his Lordship ascended a platform on the north side of
     the monument,
And the bands played cheerfully till their breath was almost
     spent ;
Then his Lordship received three ringing cheers from the
     people there,
Then he requested the Rev. John M'Lean to open the
     proceedings with prayer.

And after the prayer, Major Menzies stepped forward
And said, " Ladies and gentlemen, for the Black Watch I
　　have great regard ;
And the duty I have to perform gives me great content,
And that is to ask the noble Marquis to unveil this
　　monument."

Then he handed the noble Marquis a Lochaber axe to unveil
　　the Monument,
And the Marquis said, " Sir, to your request I most willingly
　　consent."
Then he unveiled the monument in memory of the gallant
　　Forty-twa,
While the bands played up the " Highland Laddie " as loud
　　as they could blaw.

And when the bands ceased playing the noble Marquis said,
" This monument I declare is very elegantly made,
And its bold style is quite in keeping with the country I find,
And the Committee were fortunate in obtaining so able a
　　designer as Mr. Rhind."

Then, turning to the Chief Magistrate of Aberfeldy,
He said, " Sir, I have been requested by the Committee
To give you the deed conveying the monument to your care,
With the feu-charter of the ground, therefore, sir, I'd have
　　you beware."

Then the Chief Magistrate Forbes to Lord Breadalbane said,
" My noble Lord, I accept the charge, and you needn't be
　　afraid.
Really it gives me much pleasure in accepting as I now do
　　from thee
This Memorial, along with the deeds, on behalf of Aberfeldy."

Then Major Menzies proposed three cheers for the burgh of
    Aberfeldy,
And three cheers were given right heartily.
Then the Taymouth Band played " God Save the Queen,"
Then the processionists marched to the New Public School,
    happy and serene.

Then there was a banquet held in the school,
At which three hundred sat down and ate till they were full ;
And Lord Breadalbane presided, and had on his right,
Magistrates, Colonels, and Provosts, a most beautiful sight.

And the toasts of " The Queen," " Prince and Princess of
    Wales," were given,
Wishing them prosperity while they are living ;
Then the noble Chairman proposed " The Army, Navy and
    Volunteers,"
Which was loudly responded to with three loud cheers.

Then Colonel Smith, of the Highland Volunteers, from
    Bonnie Dundee,
Replied for the Volunteers right manfully.
Then the noble Chairman said, " The toast I have now to
    propose
Is long life and prosperity to the Royal Highlanders in spite
    of their foes."

Then the toast was drunk with Highland honours and hearts
    so true,
While Pipe-Major M'Dougall played " The 42nd March at
    Waterloo."
So ended the proceedings in honour of the Black Watch, the
    bravest of men,
And the company with one accord sung the National Anthem.

LOST ON THE PRAIRIE

In one of the States of America, some years ago,
There suddenly came on a violent storm of snow,
Which was nearly the death of a party of workmen,
Who had finished their day's work—nine or ten of them.

The distance was nearly twenty miles to their camp,
And with the thick falling snow their clothes felt damp,
As they set out for their camp, which was in a large grove,
And to reach it, manfully against the storm they strove.

The wind blew very hard, and the snow was falling fast,
Still, they plodded on, but felt a little downcast,
And the snow fell so fast they could scarcely see,
And they began to think they were lost on the wild prairie.

And they suddenly noticed marks of footsteps in the snow,
Which they found were their own tracks, as onward they
    did go,
Then they knew they were lost on the great prairie,
And what could they do in such a fearful extremity ?

Then their hearts began to sink with woe,
In dread of having to pass the night in the snow,
And they cried, " Oh, God! help us to find our way,
Or else we are lost on the lonely prairie."

And while they stood shivering with the cold,
One of the party a particular horse did behold,
Which was known by the name of Old Jack,
So to take off his bridle they were not slack.

When the horse was let free he threw up his head and tail,
Which seemed to say, " Follow me, and ye will not fail.
So come on, boys, and follow me,
And I'll guide ye home safely."

And they cried, " Old Jack can show us the way,
So let's follow his tracks without dismay " ;
And with the falling snow they were chilled to the bone,
But the horse seemed to say, " I'll show ye home."

And at last they gave a shout of delight
When they saw their camp fire burning bright,
Which was to them a cheerful sight,
And they caressed Old Jack for guiding them home that
    night.

And they felt thankful to God for their safety,
And they danced around Old Jack with their hearts full of glee,
And Old Jack became a favourite from that day,
Because he saved them from being lost on the wild prairie.

THE IRISH CONVICT'S RETURN

Ye mountains and glens of Old Ireland,
    I've returned home to ye again ;
During my absence from ye
    My heart always felt great pain.

Oh, how I long'd to see you dear Nora,
    And the old folks at home ;
And the beautiful Lakes o' Killarney,
    Where we oft together did roam.

Ye beautiful Lakes of Killarney,
    Ye are welcome to me again ;
I will now reform my character,
    And from all bad company refrain.

Oh, how I have long'd to see my old father
  And my mother dearer than all ;
And my favour to dog Charlie
  That wont to come at my call.

Ye green hills and lakes of Old Ireland,
  Ye are dearer than life unto me ;
Many sleepless nights I have had
  Since my banishment from thee.

But to-night I will see the old folks
  And my dear Nora too . . .
And she and I will get married,
  And I'm sure we will never rue.

And we may have plenty of children,
  And for them I will work like a man.
And I hope Nora and I will live happy,
  And do the best we can.

For my own part, I will never grumble,
  But try and be content . . .
And walk in the paths of virtue,
  And remember my banishment.

And at night at the fireside with Nora,
  I will tell her of my limbs being bound,
And all my great hardships endured,
  And how I was lash'd like a hound.

And when my story is ended,
  Nora will sympathise with her tears,
Which will help to drown my sorrow,
  And help me through coming years.

LITTLE JAMIE

Ither laddies may ha'e finer claes, and may be better fed,
But nane o' them a' has sic a bonnie curly heid,
O sic a blythe blink in their e'e,
As my ain curly fair-hair'd laddie, Little Jamie.

When I gang oot tae tak' a walk wi' him, alang the Magdalen
  Green,
It mak's my heart feel lichtsome tae see him sae sharp and
  keen,
And he pu's the wee gowans, and gie's them to me,
My ain curly fair-hair'd laddie, Little Jamie.

When he rises in the mornin' an' gets oot o' bed,
He says, mither, mind ye'll need tae toast my faither's bread.
For he aye gie's me a bawbee ;
He's the best little laddie that ever I did see,
My ain curly fair-hair'd laddie, Little Jamie.

When I gang oot tae tak' a walk alang the streets o' Dundee,
And views a' the little laddies that I chance to see,
Nane o' them a' seems sae lovely to me,
As my ain curly fair-hair'd laddie, Little Jamie.

The laddie is handsome and fair to be seen,
He has a bonnie cheerie mou', and taw blue e'en,
And he prattles like an auld grandfaither richt merrily ;
He's the funniest little laddie that ever I did see,
My ain curly fair-hair'd laddie, Little Jamie.

Whene'er that he kens I am coming hame frae my wark,
He runs oot tae meet me as cheerful as the lark,
And he says, faither, I'm wanting just a'e bawbee,
My ain curly fair-hair'd laddie, Little Jamie.

AN ADDRESS TO THE REV. GEORGE GILFILLAN

All hail to the Rev. George Gilfillan of Dundee,
He is the greatest preacher I did ever hear or see.
He is a man of genius bright,
And in him his congregation does delight,
Because they find him to be honest and plain,
Affable in temper, and seldom known to complain.
He preaches in a plain straightforward way,
The people flock to hear him night and day,
And hundreds from the doors are often turn'd away,
Because he is the greatest preacher of the present day.
He has written the life of Sir Walter Scott,
And while he lives he will never be forgot,
Nor when he is dead,
Because by his admirers it will be often read ;
And fill their minds with wonder and delight,
And wile away the tedious hours on a cold winter's night.
He has also written about the Bards of the Bible,
Which occupied nearly three years in which he was not idle,
Because when he sits down to write he does it with might
    and main,
And to get an interview with him it would be almost vain,
And in that he is always right,
For the Bible tells us whatever your hands findeth to do,
Do it with all your might.
Rev. George Gilfillan of Dundee, I must conclude my muse,
And to write in praise of thee my pen does not refuse,
Nor does it give me pain to tell the world fearlessly, that
    when
You are dead they shall not look upon your like again.

AN ADDRESS TO SHAKESPEARE

Immortal! William Shakespeare, there's none can you excel,
You have drawn out your characters remarkably well,
Which is delightful for to see enacted upon the stage—
For instance, the love-sick Romeo, or Othello, in a rage ;
His writings are a treasure, which the world cannot repay,
He was the greatest poet of the past or of the present day—
Also the greatest dramatist, and is worthy of the name,
I'm afraid the world shall never look upon his like again.
His tragedy of Hamlet is moral and sublime,
And for purity of language, nothing can be more fine—
For instance, to hear the fair Ophelia making her moan,
At her father's grave, sad and alone. . . .
In his beautiful play, " As You Like It," one passage is very
    fine,
Just for instance in the forest of Arden, the language is
    sublime,
Where Orlando speaks of his Rosalind, most lovely and
    divine,
And no other poet I am sure has written anything more fine ;
His language is spoken in the Church and by the Advocate
    at the bar,
Here and there and everywhere throughout the world afar ;
His writings abound with gospel truths, moral and sublime,
And I'm sure in my opinion they are surpassing fine ;
In his beautiful tragedy of Othello, one passage is very fine,
Just for instance where Cassio looses his lieutenancy
. . . By drinking too much wine ;
And in grief he exclaims, " Oh! that men should put an
Enemy in their mouths to steal away their brains."
In his great tragedy of Richard the III., one passage is very
    fine

Where the Duchess of York invokes the aid of the Divine
For to protect her innocent babes from the murderer's
    uplifted hand,
And smite him powerless, and save her babes, I'm sure 'tis
    really grand.
Immortal! Bard of Avon, your writings are divine,
And will live in the memories of your admirers until the end
    of time ;
Your plays are read in family circles with wonder and
    delight,
While seated around the fireside on a cold winter's night.

THE FAIR MAID OF PERTH'S HOUSE

All ye good people, afar and near,
To my request pray lend an ear ;
I advise you all without delay to go
And see the Fair Maid's House—it is a rare show.

Some of the chairs there are very grand,
They have been cut and carved by a skilful hand ;
And kings, perchance, if the truth were told,
Have sat on them in days of old.

King James the First of Scotland was murdered there,
And his cries for mercy rent the air.
But the Highland robbers only laughed at him,
And murdered him in the dungeon and thought it no sin.

Then there's an ancient shrine upstairs,
Where the Monks and Saints said their prayers,
To the Holy Virgin, be it told ;
And the house, it is said, is six hundred years old.

The old cruisie lamps are there to be seen,
Which let the monks see to write from their sheen,
And if the walls could speak, they could tell a fearful tale,
Which would make the people's cheeks turn pale.

Then there's an old claymore dug up from Culloden Moor,
Which in its time shed innocent blood, I am sure,
If not at Culloden Moor, some other place,
Which no doubt the truth of it history might trace.

The interior of the house is magnificent to be seen,
And the wood panelling, I'm sure, would please the Queen ;
And the old fire-place, with its big fire,
Is all that visitors could desire.

Then there's a ring in a big stone near by the door,
Where gentlemen tethered their horses in days of yore ;
And on the staircase door there's a tirling pin
For making a rattling noise when anyone wanted in.

The mistress of the house is very kind,
A more affable woman would be hard to find ;
And to visitors she is very good,
And well versed in history, be it understood.

THE QUEEN'S DIAMOND JUBILEE

CELEBRATIONS

'Twas in the year of 1897, and on the 22nd of June,
Her Majesty's Diamond Jubilee in London caused a great
    boom ;
Because high and low came from afar to see,
The grand celebrations at Her Majesty's Diamond Jubilee.

People were there from almost every foreign land,
Which made the scene really imposing and grand ;
Especially the Queen's carriage, drawn by eight cream-
    coloured bays,
And when the spectators saw it joyous shouts they did
    raise.

Oh! it was a most gorgeous sight to be seen,
Numerous foreign magnates were there for to see the Queen ;
And to the vast multitude there of women and men,
Her Majesty for two hours showed herself to them.

The head of the procession looked very grand—
A party of the Horse Guards with their gold-belaced band ;
Which also headed the procession of the Colonial States,
While slowly they rode on until opposite the Palace gates.

Then the sound of the National Anthem was heard quite
    clear,
And the sound the hearts of the mighty crowd it did cheer ;
As they heard the loyal hymning on the morning air,
The scene was most beautiful and surpassing fair.

On the house tops thousands of people were to be seen,
All in eager expectation of seeing the Queen ;
And all of them seemed to be happy and gay,
Which enhanced the scene during the day.

And when Field Marshal Roberts in the procession passed by,
The cheers from thousands of people arose very high ;
And to see him on his war horse was inspiring to see,
Because he rode his charger most splendidly.

The Natal mounted troops were loudly cheered, they looked
    so grand,
And also the London Irish Emerald Isle Band ;
Oh it was a most magnificent sight to see.
The Malta Militia and Artillery,
And the Trinidad Artillery, and also bodies of infantry,
And, as the crowd gazed thereon, it filled their hearts with
    glee.

Her Majesty looked well considering her years,
And from the vast crowd burst forth joyous cheers ;
And Her Majesty bowed to the shouts of acclamation,
And smiled upon the crowd with a loving look of admiration.

His Excellency Chan Yin Hun in his carriage was a great
    attraction,
And his Oriental garb seemed to give the people great
    satisfaction ;
While the two little Battenberg's carriage, as it drove along,
Received from the people cheering loud and long.

And when the Dragoon Guards and the Hussars filed past
    at the walk,
Then loudly in their praise the people did talk ;
And the cavalry took forty minutes to trot past,
While the spectators in silent wonder stood aghast.

Her Majesty the Empress Frederick a great sensation made,
She was one of the chief attractions in the whole cavalcade ;
And in her carriage was the Princess Louise, the Marchioness
    of Lorne,
In a beautiful white dress, which did per person adorn.

The scene in Piccadilly caused a great sensation,
The grand decorations there were the theme of admiration ;
And the people in St. James Street were taken by
　　surprise,
Because the lovely decorations dazzled their eyes

The 42nd Highlanders looked very fine,
When they appeared and took up a position on the line ;
And the magnificent decorations in the Strand,
As far east as the Griffin was attractive and grand.

And the grandstand from Buckingham Palace to Temple
　　Bar,
Was crowded with eager eyes from afar,
Looking on the floral decorations and flags unfurled,
Which has been the grandest spectacle ever seen in the
　　world.

The corner building of St. James Street side was lovely to
　　view,
Ornamented with pink and white bunting and a screen of
　　blue ;
And to the eye, the inscription thereon most beautiful
　　seems :
" Thou art alone the Queen of earthly Queens."

The welcome given to Commander-in-Chief Lord Wolseley
　　was very flattering,
The people cheered him until the streets did ring ;
And the foreign princes were watched with rivetted
　　admiration,
And caused among the sight-seers great consternation.

And private householders seemed to vie with each
    other,
In the lavishness of their decorations, and considered it no
    bother ;
And never before in the memory of man,
Has there been a national celebration so grand.

And in conclusion, I most earnestly do pray,
May God protect Her Majesty for many a day ;
My blessing on her noble form and on her lofty head,
And may she wear a crown of glory hereafter when dead.

AN ODE TO THE QUEEN

All hail to the Empress of India, Great Britain's Queen!
Long may she live in health, happy and serene ;
    Loved by her subjects at home and abroad ;
Blest may she be when lying down
    To sleep, and rising up, by the Eternal God ;
Happy may her visions be in sleep . . .
    And happy her thoughts in the day time ;
Let all loyal subjects drink to her health
    In a flowing bumper of Rhenish Wine.
And when the final hour shall come to summon her away,
May her soul be wafted to the realms of bliss,
    I most sincerely do pray, to sing with saints above,
Where all is joy, peace and love—
        In Heaven, for evermore to reign,
        God Save the Queen.   Amen.

THE DEATH OF THE QUEEN

Alas! our noble and generous Queen Victoria is dead,
And I hope her soul to Heaven has fled,
To sing and rejoice with saints above,
Where all is joy, peace, and love.

'Twas on January 22, 1901, in the evening she died at 6.30
    o'clock,
Which to the civilised world has been a great shock ;
She was surrounded by her children and grandchildren dear,
And for the motherly, pious Queen they shed many a tear.

She has been a model and faithful Queen,
Very few like her have been ;
She has acted virtuously during her long reign,
And I'm afraid the world will never see her like again.

And during her reign she was beloved by the high and the
    low,
And through her decease the people's hearts are full of woe,
Because she was kind to her subjects at home and abroad,
And now she's receiving her reward from the Eternal God.

And during her reign in this world of trouble and strife
Several attempts were made to take her life ;
Maclean he tried to shoot her, but he did fail,
But he was arrested and sent to an asylum, which made him
    bewail.

Victoria was a noble Queen, the people must confess,
She was most charitable to them while in distress ;
And in her disposition she wasn't proud nor vain,
And tears for her loss will fall as plentiful as rain.

The people around Balmoral will shed many tears
Owing to her visits amongst them for many years ;
She was very kind to the old, infirm women there,
By giving them provisions and occasionally a prayer.

And while at Balmoral she found work for men unemployed,
Which made the hearts of the poor men feel overjoyed ;
And for Her Majesty they would have laid down their lives,
Because sometimes she saved them from starving, and their
    wives.

Many happy days she spent at Balmoral,
Viewing the blooming heather and the bonnie Highland
    floral,
Along with Prince Albert, her husband dear,
But alas! when he died she shed many a tear.

She was very charitable, as everybody knows,
But the loss of her husband caused her many woes,
Because he cheered her at Balmoral as they the heather trod,
But I hope she has met him now at the Throne of God.

They ascended the Hill of Morven when she was in her
    fortieth year,
And Her Majesty was delighted as she viewed the Highland
    deer ;
Also dark Lochnagar, which is most beautiful to see,
Not far from Balmoral and the dark River Dee.

I hope they are walking in Heaven together as they did in life
In the beautiful celestial regions, free from all strife,
Where God's family together continually meet,
Where the streets are paved with gold, and everything
    complete.

Alas! for the loss of Queen Victoria the people will mourn,
But she unto them can never return ;
Therefore to mourn for her is all in vain,
Knowing that she can never return again.

Therefore, good people, one and all,
Let us be prepared for death when God does on us call,
Like the good and noble Queen Victoria of renown,
The greatest and most virtuous Queen that ever wore a
  crown.

A HUMBLE HEROINE

'Twas at the Seige of Matagarda, during the Peninsular War,
That a Mrs Reston for courage outshone any man there by
  far ;
She was the wife of a Scottish soldier in Matagarda Fort,
And to attend to her husband she there did resort.

'Twas in the Spring of the year 1810,
That General Sir Thomas Graham occupied Matagarda with
  150 men ;
These consisted of a detachment from the Scots Brigade,
And on that occasion they weren't in the least afraid.

And Captain Maclaine of the 94th did the whole of them
  command,
And the courage the men displayed was really grand ;
Because they held Matagarda for fifty-four days,
Against o'erwhelming numbers of the French—therefore
  they are worthy of praise.

The British were fighting on behalf of Spain,
But if they fought on their behalf they didn't fight in vain ;
For they beat them manfully by land and sea,
And from the shores of Spain they were forced to flee.

Because Captain Maclaine set about repairing the old fort,
So as to make it comfortable for his men to resort ;
And there he kept his men at work day by day,
Filling sand-bags and stuffing them in the walls without delay.

There was one woman in the fort during those trying days,
A Mrs Reston, who is worthy of great praise ;
She acted like a ministering angel to the soldiers while there,
By helping them to fill sand-bags, it was her constant care.

Mrs Reston behaved as fearlessly as any soldier in the
    garrison,
And amongst the soldiers golden opinions she won,
For her presence was everywhere amongst the men,
And the service invaluable she rendered to them.

Methinks I see that brave heroine carrying her child,
Whilst the bullets were falling around her, enough to drive
    her wild ;
And bending over it to protect it from danger,
Because to war's alarms it was a stranger.

And while the shells shrieked around, and their fragments
    did scatter,
She was serving the men at the guns with wine and water ;
And while the shot whistled around, her courage wasn't
    slack,
Because to the soldiers she carried sand-bags on her back.

62

A little drummer boy was told to fetch water from the well,
But he was afraid because the bullets from the enemy
    around it fell ;
And the Doctor cried to the boy, Why are you standing
    there ?
But Mrs Reston said, Doctor, the bairn is feared, I do
    declare.

And she said, Give me the pail, laddie, I'll fetch the water,
Not fearing that the shot would her brains scatter ;
And without a moment's hesitation she took the pail,
Whilst the shot whirred thick around her, yet her courage
    didn't fail.

And to see that heroic woman the scene was most grand,
Because as she drew the water a shot cut the rope in her
    hand ;
But she caught the pail with her hand dexterously,
Oh! the scene was imposing and most beautiful to see.

The British fought bravely, as they are always willing to do,
Although their numbers were but few ;
So they kept up the cannonading with their artillery,
And stood manfully at their guns against the enemy.

And five times the flagstaff was shot away,
And as often was it replaced without dismay ;
And the flag was fastened to an angle of the wall,
And the British resolved to defend it whatever did befall.

So the French were beaten and were glad to run,
And the British for defeating them golden opinions have won
All through brave Captain Maclaine and his heroes bold,
Likewise Mrs Reston, whose name should be written in;
    letters of gold.

NORA, THE MAID OF KILLARNEY

Down by the beautiful Lakes of Killarney,
Oft times I have met my own dear Barney,
In the sweet summer time of the year,
In the silvery moonlight so clear,
I've rambled with my sweetheart Barney,
Along the green banks of the Lakes of Killarney.

The Lakes of Killarney are most lovely to be seen
In the summer season when nature's face is green,
Especially in the beautiful silvery moonlight,
When its waters do shine like silver bright ;
Such was the time when me and my Barney
Went to walk by the purty Lakes of Killarney.

My Barney was beautiful, gallant, and gay,
But, alas, he has left me and gone far away,
To that foreign country called Amerikay ;
But when he returns we will get married without delay,
And again we will roam by the Lakes of Killarney,
Me and my sweetheart, charming Barney.

And until he returns I will feel rather sad,
For while walking with Barney I always felt glad ;
May God send him home again safe to me,
And he will fill my sad heart with glee,
While we walk by the Lakes of Killarney.

I dreamt one night I was walking with Barney,
Down by the beautiful Lakes of Killarney,
And he said, " Nora, dear Nora, don't fret for me,
For I will soon come home to thee ;
And I will build a nice cabin near the Lakes of Killarney,
And Nora will live happy with her own dear Barney."

But, alas, I awoke from my beautiful dream,
For, och, it was a most lovely scene ;
But I hope it will happen some unexpected day,
When Barney comes home from Amerikay ;
Then Barney will relate his adventures to me,
As we walk by the silvery Lakes of Killarney.

We will ramble among its green trees and green bushes,
And hear the sweet songs of the blackbirds and thrushes,
And gaze on its lovely banks so green,
And its waters glittering like crystal in the moonlight's
　　　sheen ;
Och! how I long to be walking with Barney,
Along the green banks of the Lakes of Killarney.

Of all the spots in Ireland, Killarney for me,
For 'twas there I first met my dear Barney :
He was singing, I remember, right merrily ;
And his singing filled my heart with glee,
And he said, " Nora, dear Nora, will you walk with me,
For you are the prettiest girl I ever did see."

" Now, Barney," I said, " you are just mocking me,
When you say no other girl like me you can see " ;
Then he said, " Nora, you are the only girl I do love,
And this I do swear by the saints above,
I will marry you, dear Nora, without delay,
When I come home from Amerikay."

But when Barney landed in Amerikay,
He courted another girl without dismay,
And he married her in the month of May,
And when I heard it I fainted away ;
So maidens beware of such men as Barney,
Or else they will deceive ye with their flattering blarney.

LITTLE POPEET : THE LOST CHILD

Near by the silent waters of the Mediterranean,
And at the door of an old hut stood a coloured man,
Whose dress was oriental in style and poor with wear,
While adown his furrowed cheeks ran many a tear.

And the poor coloured man seemed very discontent,
And his frief overcame him at this moment ;
And he wrung his hands in agony wild,
And he cried, " Oh! help me, great God, to find my child.

" And Ada, my dear wife, but now she is dead,
Which fills my poor heart with sorrow and dread ;
She was a very loving wife, but of her I'm bereft,
And I and my lost child are only left.

And, alas! I know not where to find my boy,
Who is dear to me and my only joy ;
But with the help of God I will find him,
And this day in search of him I will begin."

So Medoo leaves Turkey and goes to France,
Expecting to find his boy there perhaps by chance ;
And while there in Paris he was told
His boy by an Arab had been sold

To a company of French players that performed in the street,
Which was sad news to hear about his boy Popeet ;
And while searching for him and making great moan,
He was told he was ill and in Madame Mercy's Home.

Then away went Medoo with his heart full of joy,
To gaze upon the face of his long-lost boy ;
Who had been treated by the players mercilessly,
But was taken to the home of Madame Celeste.

She was a member of the players and the leader's wife,
And she loved the boy Popeet as dear as her life,
Because she had no children of her own ;
And for the poor ill-treated boy often she did moan.

And when Popeet's father visited the Home,
He was shown into a room where Popeet lay alone,
Pale and emaciated, in his little bed ;
And when his father saw he he thought he was dead.

And when Popeet saw his father he lept out of bed,
And only that his father caught him he'd been killed dead ;
And his father cried, " Popeet, my own darling boy,
Thank God I've found you, and my heart's full of joy."

Then Madame Mercy's tears fell thick and fast,
When she saw that Popeet had found his father at last ;
Then poor Popeet was taken home without delay,
And lived happy with his father for many a day.

THE LITTLE MATCH GIRL

It was biting cold, and the falling snow,
Which filled a poor little match girl's heart with woe,
Who was bareheaded and barefooted, as she went along the
    street,
Crying, " Who'll buy my matches ?   for I want pennies to
    buy some meat! "

When she left home she had slippers on ;
But, alas! poor child, now they were gone.
For she lost both of them while hurrying across the street,
Out of the way of two carriages which were near by her feet.

So the little girl went on, while the snow fell thick and fast ;
And the child's heart felt cold and downcast,
For nobody had bought any matches that day,
Which filled her little mind with grief and dismay.

Alas! she was hungry and shivering with cold ;
So in a corner between two houses she made bold
To take shelter from the violent storm.
Poor little waif! wishing to herself she'd never been born.

And she grew colder and colder, and feared to go home
For fear of her father beating her ; and she felt woe-begone
Because she could carry home no pennies to buy bread,
And to go home without pennies she was in dread.

The large flakes of snow covered her ringlets of fair hair ;
While the passers-by for her had no care,
As they hurried along to their homes at a quick pace,
While the cold wind blew in the match girl's face.

As night wore on her hands were numb with cold,
And no longer her strength could her uphold,
When an idea into her little head came :
She'd strike a match and warm her hands at the flame.

And she lighted the match, and it burned brightly,
And it helped to fill her heart with glee ;
And she thought she was sitting at a stove very grand ;
But, alas! she was found dead, with a match in her hand!

Her body was found half-covered with snow,
And as the people gazed thereon their hearts were full of woe;
And many present let fall a burning tear
Because she was found dead on the last night of the year,

In that mighty city of London, wherein is plenty of gold—
But, alas! their charity towards street waifs is rather cold.
But I hope the match girl's in Heaven, beside her Saviour
    dear,
A bright reward for all the hardships she suffered here.

A TALE OF ELSINORE

A little child stood thinking, sorrowfully and ill at ease,
In a forest beneath the branches of the tall pine trees—
And his big brown eyes with tears seemed dim,
While one soft arm rested on a huge dog close by him.

And only four summers had passed o'er his baby head,
And, poor little child, his twin brother was dead,
Who had died but a few days before,
And now he must play alone, for he'd see him no more.

And for many generations 'tis said for a truth
That the eldest born of the Cronberg family died early in
    youth,
Owing to a curse that pursued them for many a day,
Because the Cronberg chief had carried a lovely maiden
    away,

That belonged, 'tis said, to the bold Viking chief,
And her aged mother could find no relief ;
And she cursed the Cronberg family in accents wild,
For the loss of her darling, beautiful child.

So at last the little child crept back to its home,
And entered the silent nursery alone,
Where he knew since morning his twin brother had lain,
But, alas! they would never walk hand in hand again.

And, pausing breathless, he gazed into the darkened room,
And there he saw in the dark gloom
The aged Gudrun keeping her lonely watch o'er the dead,
Sad and forlorn at the head of the bed.

Then little Olaf sprang joyfully into the room,
And bounding upon the bed, not fearing the corpse in the
    gloom ;
And crept close beside the white form,
That was wont to walk by his side night and morn.

And with his dimpled hands his brother he did stroke,
And with grief his little heart almost broke ;
And he whispered in baby talk his brother's name,
But, alas! to him no answer came.

But his good old nurse let little Olaf be,
The more it was very sad to see ;
But she could not check the child, nor on him frown,
And as she watched him, the tears came trickling down.

Then Olaf cried, " Oh, nursey, when will he speak again ? "
And old Gudrun said, " My lamb, 'tis all in vain,
He is singing sweet songs with the angels now,"
And kissed him fondly on cheek and brow.

And the same evening, Olaf wandered out on the green,
Which to him and his brother oft a playground had been ;
And lying down on the mossy bank, their old play place,
He fell asleep with a heavenly smile upon his face.

And as he slept it seemed to him an angel drew near,
And bending o'er him seemed to drop a tear,
And swept his closed eyes with her downy wing,
Then in whispers softly she did sing—

" Love God and be good to all, and one day
You'll meet your brother in Heaven in grand array,
On that bright and golden happy shore,
Where you and your brother shall part no more."

Then the angel kissed him and vanished away,
And Olaf started to his feet in great dismay ;
Then he turned his eyes to Heaven, for his heart felt sore,
And from that day the house of Cronberg was cursed no
    more.

THE BONNIE SIDLAW HILLS

Bonnie Clara, will you go to the bonnie Sidlaw hills
And pu' the blooming heather, and drink from their rills?
There the cranberries among the heather grow,
Believe me, dear Clara, as black as the crow.

Chorus—

Then, bonnie Clara, will you go
And wander with me to and fro?
And with joy our hearts will o'erflow
When we go to the bonnie Sidlaws O.

And the rabbits and hares sport in mirthful glee
In the beautiful woods of Glen Ogilvy,
And innocent trout do sport and play
In the little rivulet of Glen Ogilvy all the day.

Chorus—

And in the bonnie woods of Sidlaw the blackbird doth sing,
Making the woodlands with his notes to ring,
Which ought to make a dull heart feel gay,
And help to cheer us on our way.

Chorus—

And there the innocent sheep are to be seen
Browsing on the purple heather and pastures green;
And the shepherd can be heard shouting to his dog
As he chases the sheep from out of the bog.

Chorus—

And from the tops of the Sidlaws can be seen
The beautiful Howe of Strathmore with its trees and
　　　shrubberies green ;
Likewise Lochee and its spinning mills
Can be seen on a clear day from the Sidlaw hills.

Chorus—

Therefore, bonnie Clara, let's away
To Sidlaw hills without delay,
And pu' the cranberries and bonnie blooming heather
While we wander to and fro on the Sidlaws together.

Chorus—

There the lovers can enjoy themselves free from care
By viewing the hilly scenery and inhaling the fresh air,
And return home at night with their hearts full of glee
After viewing the beauties of the Sidlaw hills and Glen
　　　Ogilvy.

Chorus—

BONNIE CALLANDER

Chorus—

Bonnie Helen, will you go to Callander with me
And gaze upon its beauties and romantic scenery ?
Dear Helen, it will help to drive all sorrow away ;
Therefore come, sweet Helen, and let's have a holiday.

Callander is a pretty little town most lovely to see,
Situated in the midst of mountains towering frowningly;
And Ben Ledi is the chief amongst them and famous in
　　　history,
Looking stern and rugged in all its majesty.

Chorus—

And as for Bracklinn Falls, they are impressive to sight,
Especially the Keltie, which will the visitor's heart delight,
With its bonnie banks bordered with beautiful trees,
And the effect would be sure the spectator to please.

Chorus—

The hawthorn hedges and the beautiful wild flowers
Will help to enliven the scene and while away the hours ;
And as the spectator gazes upon Keltie waterfall,
The rumbling and tumbling of the water does his heart appal.

Chorus—

As it makes one fearful plunge into a yawning abyss below,
Fifty or sixty feet beneath, where it splashes to and fro,
And seethes and boils in a great deep pool,
And the sweet, fragrant air around it is very cool.

Chorus—

'Tis said two lovers met there with a tragic fate.
Alas! poor souls, and no one near to extricate.
The rail of the bridge upon which they were leaning gave
way,
And they were drowned in the boiling gulf. Oh, horror and
dismay!

Chorus—

The Pass of Leny is most wild and amazing to see,
With its beetling crags and towering mountains and romantic
scenery ;

74

And the brawling Leny, with its little waterfalls,
Will repay the visitor for the time occupied any time he calls.

Chorus—

Then lovers of the picturesque make haste and go away
To the pretty little village of Callander without delay,
And breathe the fresh air in the harvest time,
And revel amongst romantic scenery in the beautiful
     sunshine.

BONNIE KILMANY

Bonnie Kilmany, in the County of Fife,
Is a healthy spot to reside in to lengthen one's life.
The scenery there in the summer time is truly grand,
Especially the beautiful hills and the woodland.

Chorus—

    Then, bonnie Annie, will you go with me
    And leave the crowded city of Dundee,
    And breathe the pure, fragrant air
    In the Howe of Kilmany, so lovely and fair ?

And the little village in the Howe is lovely to see,
In the midst of green trees and shrubbery ;
And the little rivulet, as it wimples along,
Can be heard singing aloud an aquatic song.

Chorus—

And the old church there is built on a knoll,
And on the Sabbath mornings the church bell does toll,
Inviting the people to join in prayer,
While the echoes of the bell is heard in mid-air.

Chorus—

Then there's a little schoolroom, surrounded by trees,
A favourite haunt for butterflies and busy bees,
And an old red-tiled smithy near by,
And the clink of the hammers can be heard sounding high.

Chorus—

And there's a wood sawmill by the roadway,
And the noise can be heard by night and day,
As the circular saw wheels round and round,
Making the village with its echoes resound.

Chorus—

And in the harvest time on a fine summer morn
The Howe looks most beautiful when the corn is shorn ;
And to hear the beautiful lark singing on high
Will make you exclaim, " Dull care, good-bye."

Chorus—

BONNIE MONTROSE

Beautiful town of Montrose, I will now commence my lay,
And I will write in praise of thee without dismay ;
And, in spite of all your foes,
I will venture to call thee Bonnie Montrose.

Your Chain Bridge is most magnificent to be seen,
Spanning the River Esk, a beautiful tidal stream,
Which abounds with beautiful trout and salmon,
And can be had for the catching without any gammon.

Then as for the Mid Links, it is most charming to be seen,
And I'm sure it's a very nice bowling green ;
There the people can enjoy themselves and inhale pure air
Emanating from the sea and beautiful flowers there.

And as for the High Street, it's most beautiful to see,
There's no street can surpass it in the town of Dundee,
Because it is so long and wide
That the people can pass on either side
Without jostling one another
Or going to any bother.

Beautiful town of Montrose near by the seaside,
With your fine ships and streets so wide ;
'Tis health for the people that in you reside,
Because they inhale the pure, fragrant air
Emanating from the sea waves and shrubberies there ;
And the inhabitants of Montrose ought to feel gay
Because you are one of the bonniest towns in Scotland at the
    present day.

BEAUTIFUL COMRIE

AND ITS SURROUNDINGS

Ye lovers of the picturesque, away, away!
To beautiful Comrie and have a holiday ;
And bask in the sunshine and inhale the fragrant air
Emanating from the woodlands and shrubberies there.

The charming village of Comrie is most lovely to be seen,
Especially in the summer season when the trees are green ;
And near by is Loch Earn and its waters sparkling clear,
And as the tourist gazes thereon his spirits it will cheer.

Then St. Fillans is a beautiful spot, I must confess,
It is really a picture of rural loveliness;
Because out of the quiet lake the river ripples merrily,
And all round are hills beautiful in shape and nothing
    uncomely.

The rocky knoll to the south is a most seductive place,
And in the hotel there visitors will find every solace ;
And the flower-decked cottages are charming to see,
Also handsome villas suitable for visitors of high and low
    degree.

Then there's St. Fillan's Hill, a prehistoric fort,
And visitors while there to it should resort ;
And to the tourist the best approach is from the west,
Because in climbing the hill his strength it will test.

78

And descending the hill as best one may,
The scene makes the tourist's heart feel gay ;
And by the west side is reached a wooded dell,
And about two hundred yards from that there's St. Fillan's
Well.

Oh, charming Comrie! I must conclude my lay,
And to write in praise of thee I virtually do say
That your lovely mountains and silver birches will drive dull
care away :
Therefore lovers of the picturesque, away, away!

To beautiful Comrie and have a holiday,
And I'm sure you will return with spirits light and gay,
After viewing the Sylvan beauties and hoary beeches there,
Also pines, ferns, and beautiful oaks, I do declare.

BEAUTIFUL NORTH BERWICK

AND ITS SURROUNDINGS

North Berwick is a watering-place with golfing links green,
With a fine bathing beach most lovely to be seen ;
And there's a large number of handsome villas also,
And often it's called the Scarborough of Scotland, as
Portobello.

The greatest attraction is Tantallon Castle, worthy of
regard,
About three miles distant to the eastward ;
Which in time of war received many a shock,
And it's deemed impregnable and built on a perpendicular
rock.

The castle was built in times unknown to history,
But 'tis said it belonged to the Douglas family ;
And the inside is a labyrinth of broken staircases,
Also ruined chambers and many dismal places.

Then there's the Berwick Law Hill, 612 feet high,
Which no doubt is very attractive to the eye,
And skirted with a wood and a public walk,
Where visitors can enjoy themselves and have a social talk.

The wood is really lovely and enchanting to be seen,
In the spring or summer season when the trees are green ;
And as ye listen to the innocent birds singing merrily there,
'Twill help to elevate your spirits and drive away dull care.

Then near by Tantallon is the fishing village of Canty Bay,
Where boats can be hired to the Bass Rock, about two miles
    away ;
And the surrounding scenery is magnificent to see,
And as the tourists view the scene it fills their hearts with
    glee.

Then away! then away! pleasure-seekers in bands,
And view Gullane with its beautiful sands,
Which stretch along the sandy shores of Fife,
Where the tourist can enjoy himself and be free from strite·

BEAUTIFUL CRIEFF

Ye lovers of the picturesque, if ye wish to drown your grief,
Take my advice, and visit the ancient town of Crieff ;
The climate is bracing, and the walks lovely to see.
Besides, ye can ramble over the district, and view the
    beautiful scenery.

The town is admirably situated from the cold winter winds,
And the visitors, during their stay there, great comfort finds,
Because there is boating and fishing, and admission free,
Therefore they can enjoy themselves right merrily.

There is also golf courses, tennis greens, and good roads,
Which will make the travelling easier to tourists with great
    loads,
And which will make the bicyclists' hearts feel gay,
Because they have everything there to make an enjoyable
    holiday.

The principal river there is the Earn, rolling on its way,
And which flows from Loch Earn, and joins the silvery Tay
Above Newburgh, after a course of more than thirty miles ;
And as the tourist views the scene with joy he smiles.

The princely domain of Drummond Castle is most beautiful
    to be seen,
Especially when the woody landscape is blown full green,
And from the entrance gate to the castle an avenue extends
    all the way,
And to view the branches of the trees interlacing makes the
    heart feel gay.

Drummond Castle's flowery gardens are really very grand ;
They cannot be surpassed in Great Britain,
And in the summer-time the bee and the butterfly are there
    on the wing,
And with the carolling of birds the gardens doth ring.

And from Knock Hill on the north and west,
The view from its summit is considered the best ;
Because the Grampians and the Ochils can be seen,
While the beautiful rich fertile valley lies between.

And there are many seats where the weary traveller can rest,
And there is also a fountain of water, the very best,
While visitors can drink of while resting there,
And gaze on the magnificent scenery and inhale the pure air.

Then there's Lady Mary's Walk near the Bridge of
    Turret,
Which I hope visitors will go and see and not forget,
Because near by grows a magnificent oak most lovely
    to see,
Which is known by the name of Eppie Callum's Tree.

And at each end of this walk the visitors can ascend Laggan
    Hill,
And as they view the woods and fields with joy their hearts
    will thrill ;
And they will find seats plenteous on this elevated bower,
On which they may rest and wile away the hour.

The Hydropathic is situated on an eminence most grand,
And is one of the largest buildings in fair Scotland ;
And capable of accommodating five hundred visitors, who
    often call there,
To recuperate their health and breathe the fragrant air.

Then there's Abercairny, which is most beautiful to view,
And Her Majesty the Queen visited the grounds in 1842 ;
And the park and the trees has the aspect of a southern
    scene,
And the lovely appearance of it gladdened the heart of our
    Queen.

Then there's the village of Foulis, which tourists ought to
    see,
Because the scenery there is charming and pretty ;
And there's a sycamore tree there that was planted 300 years
    ago,
And I'm sure the sight thereof will please both high and low.

Therefore, in conclusion, to all lovers of the beautiful I will
    say,
If ye really wish to spend an enjoyable holiday,
I would recommend Crieff for lovely scenery and pure air ;
Besides, the climate gives health to many visitors during
    their stay there.

BEAUTIFUL BALMORAL

Ye lovers of the picturesque, away and see
Beautiful Balmoral, near by the River Dee ;
There ye will see the deer browsing on the heathery hills,
While adown their sides run clear sparkling rills.

Which the traveller can drink of when he feels dry,
And admire the dark River Dee near by,
Rolling smoothly and silently on its way,
Which is most lovely to see on a summer day.

There the trout do sport and play
During the live-long summer day ;
Also plenty of salmon are there to be seen,
Glittering like silver in the sun's sheen.

And the mountains are rugged and wild to be seen,
But the woodlands are beautiful when Nature's face is green;
There numerous rabbits do gambol all day
Amongst the green shrubbery all lively and gay.

There's one charming spot most magnificent to be seen,
'Tis Balmoral Castle, the Highland Home of our Queen ;
The surrounding scenery is enchanting to see,
While near by rolls past the lovely River Dee.

Therefore, ye lovers of the picturesque, away and see
Beautiful Balmoral Castle and its grand scenery,
And the sight will fill your hearts with glee,
As ye walk along the bonnie banks o' the River Dee.

THE BEAUTIFUL VILLAGE OF PENICUIK

The village of Penicuik, with its neighbouring spinning mills,
Is most lovely to see, and the Pentland Hills ;
And though of a barren appearance and some parts steep,
They are covered with fine pasture and sustain flocks of
    sheep.

There, tourists while there should take a good look,
By viewing the surrounding beauties of Penicuik ;
About three miles south-west is the romantic locality
Of Newhall, which is most fascinating and charming to see.

Then about half a mile above Newhall the River Esk is seen,
Which sparkles like crystal in the sun's sheen ;
And on the Esk there's a forking ridge forming a linn
Betwixt two birch trees, which makes a noisy din.

And on a rocky protuberance close by is Mary Stuart's bower
Where Scotland's ill-starred Queen spent many an hour,
Which is composed of turf and a nice round seat
Commanding a full view of the linn—the sight is quite a
    treat.

Then there's Habbie's Howe, where the beauties of summer
    grow,
Which cannot be excelled in Scotland for pastoral show ;
'Tis one of the most beautiful landscapes in fair Scotland,
For the scenery there is most charming and grand.

Then ye tourists to the village of Penicuik haste away,
And there spend the lovely summer day
By climbing the heathy, barren Pentland Hills,
And drink the pure water from their crystal rills.

BEAUTIFUL NAIRN

All ye tourists who wish to be away
From the crowded city for a brief holiday ;
The town of Nairn is worth a visit, I do confess,
And it's only about fifteen miles from Inverness.

And in the summer season it's a very popular bathing-place,
And the visitors from London and Edinburgh finds solace,
As they walk along the yellow sand beach inhaling fresh air ;
Besides, there's every accommodation for ladies and gentle-
    men there.

Then there's a large number of bathing coaches there,
And the climate is salubrious, and very warm the air ;
And every convenience is within the bathers' reach,
Besides, there's very beautiful walks by the sea beach.

The visitors to Nairn can pass away the time agreeably,
By viewing Tarbetness, which slopes downwards to the sea ;
And Queen Street is one of the prettiest thoroughfares,
Because there's splendid shops in it, and stocked with
    different wares.

And there's ornamental grounds, and lovely shady nooks,
Which is a great advantage to visitors while reading their
    books ;
And there's a certain place known as the Ladies' Beach,
So private that no intruder can them reach.

And there's many neat cottages with gardens very nice,
And picturesque villas, which can be rented at a reasonable
price ;
Besides, there's a golf course for those that such a game seeks,
Which would prove a great attraction to the knights of clubs
and cleeks.

The surrounding scenery of Nairn is magnificent to be seen,
Especially its fertile fields and woodlands so green ;
Besides, not far from Nairn, there's Cawdor Castle, the
ancient seat
Of the noble Thanes of Cawdor, with its bold turrets so neat.

And its massive proportions is very imposing to see,
Because the arched entrance is secured by a drawbridge and
a fosse ;
And visitors will be allowed all over the grounds to roam,
Besides shown over the castle if the Earl is not at home.

The scenery surrounding the castle is charming in the
summer-time,
And the apples in the orchard there is very fine,
Also the flower-beds are most beautiful to see,
Especially in the month of June, when the birds sing merrily.

Then there's the ancient stronghold of the Hays of Lochloy,
And visitors when they see it will it heartily enjoy ;
And a little further on there's the blasted heath of Macbeth,
And a hillock where the witches are wont to dance till out
of breath.

And as the visitors to Nairn walk along the yellow sand,
They can see, right across the Moray Firth, the Black Island
    so grand,
With its productive fields and romantic scenery,
And as the tourist gazes thereon his heart fills with ecstasy.

And Darnaway Castle is well worthy of praise,
And to oblige all visitors there are open days,
When they can see the castle where one thousand warriors
    in all
Oft have assembled in the Earl of Randolph's Hall.

And in conclusion I will say for good bathing Nairn is the
    best,
And besides its pleasant scenery is of historical interest ;
And the climate gives health to many visitors while there,
Therefore I would recommend Nairn for balmy pure air.

BEAUTIFUL TORQUAY

All ye lovers of the picturesque, away
To beautiful Torquay and spend a holiday ;
'Tis health for invalids for to go there
To view the beautiful scenery and inhale the fragrant air,
Especially in the winter and spring-time of the year,
When the weather is not too hot, but is balmy and clear.

Torquay lies in a very deep and well-sheltered spot,
And at first sight by strangers it won't be forgot ;
'Tis said to be the mildest place in all England,
And surrounded by lofty hills most beautiful and grand.

'Twas here that William of Orange first touched English
    ground,
And as he viewed the beautiful spot his heart with joy did
    rebound ;
And an obelisk marks the spot where he did stand,
And which for long will be remembered throughout England.

Torquay, with its pier and its diadem of white,
Is a most beautiful and very dazzling sight,
With its white villas glittering on the sides of its green hills,
And as the tourist gazes thereon with joy his heart fills.

The heights around Torquay are most beautiful to be seen,
Especially when the trees and shrubberies are green,
And to see the pretty houses under the cliff is a treat,
And the little town enclosed where two deep valleys meet.

There is also a fine bathing establishment near the pier,
Where the tourist can bathe without any fear ;
And as the tourists there together doth stroll,
I advise them to visit a deep chasm called Daddy's Hole.

Then there's Bablicome, only two miles from Torquay,
Which will make the stranger's heart feel gay,
As he stands on the cliff four hundred feet above the sea,
Looking down, 'tis sure to fill his heart with ecstasy.

The lodging-houses at Bablicome are magnificent to be seen,
And the accommodation there would suit either king or
    queen,
And there's some exquisite cottages embowered in the
    woodland,
And sloping down to the sea shore, is really very grand.

You do not wonder at Napoleon's exclamation
As he stood on the deck of the " Bellerophon," in a fit of
    admiration,
When the vessel was lying to windbound,
He exclaimed—" Oh, what a beautiful country! " his joy
    was profound.

And as the tourist there in search of beautiful spots doth
    rove,
Let them not forget to enquire for Anstey's Cove,
And there they will see a beautiful beach of milky white,
And the sight will fill their hearts with delight.

Oh! beautiful Torquay, with your lovely scenery,
And your magnificent cottages sloping down to the sea,
You are the most charming spot in all England,
With your picturesque bay and villas most grand.

And, in conclusion, to tourists I will say,
Off! off to Torquay and make no delay,
For the scenery is magnificent, and salubrious the air,
And 'tis good for the health to reside there.

THE ANCIENT TOWN OF LEITH

Ancient town of Leith, most wonderful to be seen,
With your many handsome buildings, and lovely links so
    green,
And the first buildings I may mention are the Courthouse
    and Town Hall,
Also Trinity House, and the Sailors' Home of Call.

Then as for Leith Fort, it was erected in 1779, which is
    really grand,
And which is now the artillery headquarters in Bonnie
    Scotland ;
And as for the Docks, they are magnificent to see,
They comprise five docks, two piers, 1,141 yards long
    respectively.

And there's steamboat communication with London and the
    North of Scotland,
And the fares are really cheap and the accommodation most
    grand ;
Then there's many public works in Leith, such as flour mills,
And chemical works, where medicines are made for curing
    many ills.

Besides, there are sugar refineries and distilleries,
Also engineer works, saw-mills, rope-works, and breweries,
Where many of the inhabitants are daily employed,
And the wages they receive make their hearts feel over-
    joyed.

In past times Leith shared the fortunes of Edinboro',
Because it withstood nine months' siege, which caused them
    great sorrow ;
They fought against the Protestants in 1559 and in '60,
But they beat them back manfully and made them flee.

Then there's Bailie Gibson's fish shop, most elegant to be
    seen,
And the fish he sells there are beautiful and clean ;
And for himself, he is a very good man,
And to deny it there's few people can.

The suburban villas of Leith are elegant and grand,
With accommodation that might suit the greatest lady in
    the land ;
And the air is pure and good for the people's health,—
And health, I'm sure, is better by far than wealth.

The Links of Leith are beautiful for golfers to play,
After they have finished the toils of the day ;
It is good for their health to play at golf there,
On that very beautiful green, and breathe the pure air.

The old town of Leith is situated at the junction of the River
    of Leith,
Which springs from the land of heather and heath ;
And no part in the Empire is growing so rapidly,
Which the inhabitants of Leith are right glad to see.

And Leith in every way is in itself independent,
And has been too busy to attend to its own adornment ;
But I venture to say and also mention
That the authorities to the town will pay more attention.

Ancient town of Leith, I must now conclude my muse,
And to write in praise of thee my pen does not refuse,
Because the inhabitants to me have been very kind,
And I'm sure more generous people would be hard to find.

They are very affable in temper and void of pride,
And I hope God will always for them provide ;
May He shower His blessings upon them by land and sea,
Because they have always been very kind to me.

THE CITY OF PERTH

Beautiful Ancient City of Perth,
One of the fairest on the earth,
With your stately mansions and scenery most fine,
Which seems very beautiful in the summer time ;
And the beautiful silvery Tay,
Rolling smoothly on its way,
And glittering like silver in the sunshine—
And the Railway Bridge across it is really sublime.
The scenery is very beautiful when in full bloom,
It far excels the river Doon—
For the North Inch and South Inch is most beautiful to
    behold,
Where the buttercups do shine in the sunshine like gold.

And there's the Palace of Scone, most beautiful to be seen,
Near by the river Tay and the North Inch so green,
Whereon is erected the statue of Prince Albert, late husband
    of the Queen,
And also the statue of Sir Walter Scott is most beautiful to
    be seen,
Erected on the South Inch, which would please the Queen,
And recall to her memory his novels she has read—
And cause her to feel a pang for him that is dead.

Beautiful City of Perth, along the river Tay, I must conclude
    my lay,
And to write in praise of thee my heart does not gainsay,
To tell the world fearlessly, without the least dismay—
With your stately mansions and the beautiful river Tay,
You're one of the fairest Cities of the present day.

BONNIE DUNDEE IN 1878

Oh, Bonnie Dundee ! I will sing in thy praise
A few but true simple lays,
Regarding some of your beauties of the present day—
And virtually speaking, there's none can them gainsay ;
There's no other town I know of with you can compare
For spinning mills and lasses fair,
And for stately buildings there's none can excel
The beautiful Albert Institute or the Queen's Hotel,
For it is most handsome to be seen,
Where accommodation can be had for Duke, Lord or Queen,
And the four pillars of the front are made of Aberdeen
     granite, very fine,
And most beautiful does shine, just like a looking glass,
And for beauty and grandeur there's none can them surpass.
And your fine shops in Reform Street,
Very few can with them compete
For superfine goods, there's none can excel,
From Inverness to Clerkenwell.
And your Tramways, I must confess,
That they have proved a complete success,
Which I am right glad to see . . .
And a very great improvement to Bonnie Dundee.
And there's the Royal Arch, most handsome to be seen,
Erected to the memory of our Most Gracious Queen—
Most magnificent to see,
And a very great honour to the people of Dundee.
Then there's the Baxter Park, most beautiful to see,
And a great boon it is to the people of Dundee,
For there they can enjoy themselves when they are free from
     care,

By inhaling the perfumed air,
Emanating from the sweet flowers and green trees and
   shrubs there.
Oh, Bonnie Dundee! I must conclude my muse,
And to write in praise of thee, my pen does not refuse,
Your beauties that I have alluded to are most worthy to see,
And in conclusion, I will call thee Bonnie Dundee!

LOCH NESS

Beautiful Loch Ness,
The truth to express,
Your landscapes are lovely and gay,
Along each side of your waters, to Fort Augustus all the
   way,
Your scenery is romantic . . .
With rocks and hills gigantic . . .
Enough to make one frantic,
As they view thy beautiful heathery hills,
And their clear crystal rills,
And the beautiful woodlands so green,
On a fine summer day . . .
From Inverness all the way . . .
Where the deer and the roe together doth play ;
And the beautiful Falls of Foyers with its crystal spray,
As clear as the day,
Enchanting and gay,
To the traveller as he gazes thereon,
That he feels amazed with delight,
To see the water falling from such a height,
That his head feels giddy with the scene,
As he views the Falls of Foyers and the woodlands so green,

That he exclaims in an ecstasy of delight—
Oh, beautiful Loch Ness!
I must sincerely confess,
That you are the most beautiful to behold,
With your lovely landscapes and water so cold.
And as he turns from the scene, he says with a sigh—
Oh, beautiful Loch Ness! I must bid you good-bye.

A DESCRIPTIVE POEM ON THE
SILVERY TAY

Beautiful silvery Tay,
With your landscapes, so lovely and gay,
Along each side of your waters, to Perth all the way ;
No other river in the world has got scenery more fine,
Only I am told the beautiful Rhine,
Near to Wormit Bay, it seems very fine,
Where the Railway Bridge is towering above its waters
    sublime,
And the beautiful ship Mars,
With her Juvenile Tars,
Both lively and gay,
Does carelessly lie
By night and by day,
In the beautiful Bay
Of the silvery Tay.
Beautiful, beautiful! silvery Tay,
Thy scenery is enchanting on a fine summer day,
Near by Balmerino it is beautiful to behold,
When the trees are in full bloom and the cornfields seems
    like gold—

And nature's face seems gay,
And the lambkins they do play,
And the humming bee is on the wing,
It is enough to make one sing,
While they carelessly do stray,
Along the beautiful banks of the silvery Tay,
Beautiful silvery Tay, rolling smoothly on your way,
Near by Newport, as clear as the day,
Thy scenery around is charming I'll be bound . . .
And would make the heart of any one feel light and gay on a
    fine summer day,
To view the beautiful scenery along the banks of the silvery
    Tay.

THE DEN O' FOWLIS

Beautiful Den o' Fowlis, most charming to be seen
In the summer season, when your trees are green ;
Especially in the bright and clear month of June,
When your flowers and shrubberies are in full bloom.

There visitors can enjoy themselves during the holidays,
And be shaded by the trees from the sun's rays,
And admire the beautiful primroses that grow there ;
And inhale their sweet perfume that fills the air.

There the little children sport and play,
Blythe and gay during the live-long summer day,
In its beautiful green and cool shady bowers,
Chasing the bee and butterfly, and pulling the flowers.

There the Minnows loup and play ;
In the little rivulet all the day ;
Right in the hollow of that fairy-like Den,
Together in little shoals of nine or ten.

And the Mavis and Blackbird merrily sing,
Making the Den with their notes to ring ;
From high noon till sunset at night,
Filling the visitor's heart with delight.

Tis most lovely to see the trees arched overhead,
And the little rivulet rolling o'er its pebbly bed,
Ane near by is an old Meal Mill ;
Likewise an old Church and Churchyard where the dead lie
    still.

The Den is always cool in the summer time,
Because it is so closely shaded from the sunshine,
By the spreading branches of the trees,
While the murmuring of the rivulet is heard on the night
    breeze.

It is a very magnificent spot the Den o' Fowlis,
And where oft the wintry wind it howls,
Among its bare and leafless withered trees,
And with fear would almost make one's heart to freeze.

To be walking through it on a dark wintry night,
Because the bare trees seem like spectres to your sight,
And everything around seems dark and drear,
And fills the timid mind with an undefinable fear.

But in the summer season it is most lovely to see;
With its fair flowers and romantic scenery,
Where the people can enjoy themselves all the day,
In the months of July, June, or May.

There the people can drink pure water when they are dry;
From the wells of spring water in the Den near by,
Which God has provided for his creatures in that lonely spot,
And such a blessing to the people shouldn't be forgot.

THE INAUGURATION OF THE
HILL O' BALGAY

Beautiful Hill o' Balgay,
With your green trees and flowers fair,
'Tis health for the old and young
For to be walking there,
To breathe the fragrant air
Emanating from the green bushes
And beautiful flowers there,
Then they can through the burying-ground roam,
And read the epitaphs on the tombstones
Before they go home.
There the lovers can wander safe arm in arm,
For policemen are there to protect them from harm
And to watch there all day,
So that no accident can befall them
In the Hill o' Balgay.
Then there's Harry Scott's mansion,
Most beautiful to be seen,
Also the Law Hill, likewise the Magdalen Green,

And the silvery Tay,
Rolling on its way.
And the coast of Fife,
And the beautiful town of St. Andrews,
Where Cardinal Beaton lost his life ;
And to be seen on a clear summer day,
From the top of the beautiful Hill o' Balgay.
On the opening day of the Hill o' Balgay,
It was a most beautiful sight to see
Numerous bands, with flags and banners, assembled in
    Dundee,
All in grand procession, with spirits light, that day,
March'd out the Blackness Road to the Hill o' Balgay.
The Earl o' Dalhousie was there on the opening day,
Also Harry Scott, the young laird o' Balgay,
And he made a great speech to the people there,
And they applauded him with cries that rent the air.
The Earl o' Dalhousie made a fine speech in his turn,
And said there was only one thing that caus'd him to
    mourn,—
There was no protection from the rain in the Hill o' Balgay,
And he would give another five hundred pounds away
For to erect a shed for the people upon a rainy day,
To keep them dry and comfortable on the Hill o' Balgay.
Then the people applauded him with three loud cheers,
For their hearts were all opened, and flowed with joyous
    tears,
So they all dispers'd quietly with spirits light that day,
And that ended the inauguration of the Hill o' Balgay.

THE BONNIE LASS O' DUNDEE

O' a' the toons that I've been in,
   I dearly love Dundee,
It's there the bonnie lassie lives,
   The lass I love to see.
Her face is fair, broon is her hair,
   And dark blue is her e'e,
And aboon a' the lasses e'er I saw,
   There's nane like her to me—
The bonnie broon-hair'd lassie o' Bonnie Dundee.

I see her in my night dreams,
   Wi' her bonnie blue e'e,
And her face it is the fairest,
   That ever I did see ;
And aboon a' the lassies e'er I saw,
   There's nane like her to me,
For she makes my heart feel lichtsome,
   And I'm aye richt glad to see—
The bonnie broon-hair'd lassie o' Bonnie Dundee.

Her eyes, they beam with innocence,
   Most lovely for to see,
And her heart it is as free from guile,
   As a child on its mother's knee ;
And aboon a' the lasses e'er I saw,
   There's nane like her to me,
For she aye seems so happy,
   And has a blythe blink in her e'e—
The bonnie broon-hair'd lassie o' Bonnie Dundee.

The lassie is tidy in her claes,
 Baith neat and clean to see ;
And her body's sma and slender,
 And a neat foot has she ;
And aboon a' the lassies e'er I saw,
 There's nane like her to me—
The bonnie broon-hair'd lassie o' Bonnie Dundee.

She sings like the nightingale,
 Richt merrily, or a wee lintie,
Wi' its heart fou' o' glee,
 And she's as frisky as a bee ;
And aboon a' the lassies e'er I saw,
 There's nane like her to me—
The bonnie broon-hair'd lassie o' Bonnie Dundee.

The lassie is as handsome
 As the lily on the lea,
And her mou' it is as red
 As a cherry on the tree ;
And she's a' the world to me,
 The bonnie broon-hair'd lassie
Wi' the bonnie blue e'e,
 She's the joy o' my heart
And the flower o' Dundee.

THE BONNIE LASS OF RUILY

'Twas in the village of Ruily there lived a bonnie lass
With red, pouting lips which few lasses could surpass,
And her eyes were as azure the blue sky,
Which caused Donald McNeill to heave many a love sigh.

Beyond the township of Ruily she never had been,
This pretty maid with tiny feet and aged eighteen ;
And when Donald would ask her to be his wife,
" No," she would say, " I'm not going to stay here all my
    life."

" I'm sick of this life," she said to Donald one day,
" By making the parridge and carrying peats from the bog
    far away."
" Then marry me, Belle, and peats you shall never carry
    again,
And we might take a trip to Glasgow and there remain."

Then she answered him crossly, " I wish you wouldn't
    bother me,
For I'm tired of this kind of talk, as you may see."
So at last there came a steamer to Ruily one day,
So big that it almost seemed to fill the bay.

Then Belle and Effie Mackinnon came to the door with a
    start,
While Belle's red, pouting lips were wide apart ;
But when she saw the Redcoats coming ashore
She thought she had never seen such splendid men before.

One day after the steamer "Resistless" had arrived,
Belle's spirits seemed suddenly to be revived;
And as Belle was lifting peats a few feet from the door
She was startled by a voice she never heard before.

The speaker wore a bright red coat and a small cap,
And she thought to herself he is a handsome chap;
Then the speaker said, " 'Tis a fine day," and began to
    flatter,
Until at last he asked Belle for a drink of watter.

Then she glanced up at him shyly, while uneasy she did feel,
At the thought of having to hoist the peat-creel;
And she could see curly, fair hair beneath his cap,
Still, she thought to herself, he is a good-looking chap.

And his eyes were blue and sparkling as the water in the
    bay,
And he spoke in a voice that was pleasant and gay;
Then he took hold of the peat-creel as he spoke,
But Belle only laughed and considered it a joke.

Then Belle shook her head and lifted the peats on her
    back,
But he followed her home whilst to her he did crack;
And by and by she brought him a drink of watter,
While with loving words he began Belle to flatter.

And after he had drank the watter and handed back the jug,
He said, " You are the sweetest flower that's to be found in
    Ruily ";
And he touched her bare arm as he spoke,
Which proved to be sailor Harry's winning stroke.

But it would have been well for Belle had it ended there,
But it did not, for the sailor followed her, I do declare ;
And he was often at old Mackinnon's fireside,
And there for hours on an evening he would abide.

And Belle would wait on him with love-lit eyes,
While Harry's heart would heave with many love sighs.
At last, one night Belle said, " I hear you're going away."
Then Harry Lochton said, " 'Tis true, Belle, and I must
    obey.

But, my heather Belle, if you'll leave Ruily with me
I'll marry you, with your father's consent, immediately."
Then she put her arms around his neck and said, " Harry,
    I will."
Then Harry said, " You'll be a sailor's wife for good or ill."

In five days after Belle got married to her young sailor lad,
And there was a grand wedding, and old Mackinnon felt
    glad ;
And old Mackinnon slapped his son-in-law on the back
And said, " I hope good health and money you will never
    lack."

At last the day came that Harry had to go away,
And Harry said, " God bless you, Belle, by night and day ;
But you will come to Portsmouth and I will meet you there,
Remember, at the railway platform, and may God of you
    take care."

And when she arrived in Portsmouth she was amazed at the
    sight,
But when she saw Harry her heart beat with delight ;
And when the train stopped, Harry to her quickly ran,
And took her tin-box from the luggage van.

Then he took her to her new home without delay,
And the endless stairs and doors filled her heart with dismay;
But for that day the hours flew quickly past,
Because she knew she was with her Harry at last.

But there came a day when Harry was ordered away,
And he said, " My darling, I'll come back some unexpected
  day."
Then he kissed her at parting and " Farewell " he cries,
While the tears fell fast from her bonnie blue eyes.

Then when Harry went away she grew very ill,
And she cried, " If Harry stays long away this illness will
  me kill."
At last Harry came home and found her ill in bed,
And he cried, " My heather Belle, you're as pale as the
  dead."

Then she cried, " Harry, sit so as I may see your face,
Beside me here, Harry, that's just the place."
Then on his shoulder she gently dropped her head ;
Then Harry cried, " Merciful heaven, my heather Belle is
  dead! "

MARY, THE MAID OF THE TAY

Ye banks and braes o' bonnie Tay,
Whaur me and my Mary oft did stray ;
But noo she is dead and gane far away,
Sae I maun mourn for lovely Mary, the Maid o' the Tay.

The first time I met her 'twas in the month of May,
And the sun was shining bricht on the Silvery Tay ;
I asked her name and she modestly did say,
" Some fouks ca's me lovely Mary, the Maid o' the Tay."

Oh, charming Mary o' the Tay,
Queen o' my soul by nicht and day ;
But noo thou'rt gane and left me here
To weep for you, sweet Mary dear.

Oh, bonnie Mary o' the Tay,
Joy o' my heart and Queen o' May ;
With thee I aye felt happy and gay
While rambling with thee on the banks o' the Tay.

Ye banks and braes o' bonnie Tay,
With my Mary ye seemed ever gay ;
But noo ye seem baith dark and drear,
For my puir heart ye canna cheer.

My Mary was handsome and fair to be seen,
She had bonnie fair hair and twa blue een ;
And she was aye happy while we carelessly did stray
Alang the banks o' the Silvery Tay.

Oh, Mary dear, I mourn thy loss,
To me the world seems nought but dross ;
Sae I maun mourn baith nicht and day
For my lovely Mary, the Maid o' the Tay.

THE HEATHERBLEND CLUB BANQUET

'Twas on the 16th of October, in 1894,
I was invited to Inverness, not far from the seashore,
To partake of a Banquet prepared by the Heatherblend
  Club,
Gentlemen who honoured me without any hubbub.

The Banquet was held in the Gellion Hotel,
And the landlord, Mr Macpherson, treated me right
    well ;
Also the servant maids were very kind to me,
Especially the girl who polished my boots most beautiful to
  see.

The Banquet consisted of roast beef, potatoes, and red
  wine,
Also hare soup and sherry, and grapes most fine,
And baked pudding and apples, lovely to be seen,
Also rick sweet milk and delicious cream.

Mr Gossip, a noble Highlander, acted as chairman,
And when the Banquet was finished the fun began ;
And I was requested to give a poetic entertainment,
Which I gave, and which pleased them to their hearts'
  content.

And for the entertainment they did me well reward
By entitling me the Heatherblend Club Bard ;
Likewise I received an Illuminated Address,
Also a purse of silver, I honestly confess.

Mr A. J. Stewart was very kind to me,
And tried all he could to make me happy;
And several songs were sung by gentlemen there—
It was the most social gathering I've been in, I do declare.

Oh, magnificent town of Inverness!
With its lovely scenery on each side,
And your beautiful river, I must confess,
'Twould be good for one's health there to reside.

There the blackbird and the mavis doth sing,
Making the woodland with their echoes to ring;
During the months of July, May and June,
When the trees and shrubberies are in full bloom.

And to see the River Ness rolling smoothly along,
Together with the blackbird's musical song;
As the sun shines bright in the month of May,
'Twill help to drive dull care away.

And Macbeth's Castle is grand to be seen,
Situated on Castle Hill, which is beautiful and green,
'Twas there Macbeth lived in days of old,
And a great tyrant he was, be it told.

I wish the Heatherblend members every success,
Hoping God will prosper them and bless;
Long May Dame Fortune smile upon them,
For all of them I've met are kind gentlemen.

And, in conclusion, I must say
I never received better treatment in my day
Than I received from my admirers in bonnie Inverness;
This on my soul and conscience I do confess.

A SUMMARY HISTORY OF SIR WILLIAM
WALLACE

Sir William Wallace of Ellerslie,
I'm told he went to the High School in Dundee,
For to learn to read and write,
And after that he learned to fight.
While at the High School in Dundee,
The Provost's son with him did disagree,
Because Wallace he did wear a dirk,
He despised him like an ignorant stirk,
Which with indignation he keenly felt,
And told him it would become him better in his belt.

Then Wallace's blood began to boil,
Just like the serpent in its coil,
Before it leaps upon its prey ;
And unto him he thus did say :
" Proud, saucy cur, come cease your prate,
For no longer I shall wait,
For to hear you insult me,
At the High School in Dundee ;
For such insolence makes my heart to smart,
And I'll plunge my dagger in your heart."

Then his heart's blood did quickly flow,
And poor Wallace did not know where to go ;
And he stood by him until dead.
Then far from him he quickly fled,
Lamenting greatly the deed he had done,
The murdering of the Provost's son.

The scene shifts to where he was fishing one day,
Where three English soldiers met him by the way,
And they asked him to give them some fish,

And from them they would make a delicious dish.
Then Wallace gave them share of his fish,
For to satisfy their wish ;
But they seemed dissatisfied with the share they got,
So they were resolved to have all the lot.

Then Wallace he thought it was time to look out,
When they were resolved to have all his trout ;
So he swung his fishing-rod with great force round his head,
And struck one of them a blow that killed him dead ;
So he instantly seized the fallen man's sword,
And the other two fled without uttering a word.

Sir William Wallace of Ellerslie,
You were a warrior of great renown,
And might have worn Scotland's crown ;
Had it not been for Monteith, the base traitor knave,
That brought you to a premature grave ;
Yes! you were sold for English gold,
And brought like a sheep from the fold,
To die upon a shameful scaffold high,
Amidst the derisive shouts of your enemies standing by.

But you met your doom like a warrior bold,
Bidding defiance to them that had you sold,
And bared your neck for the headsman's stroke ;
And cried, " Marion, dear, my heart is broke ;
My lovely dear, I come to thee,
Oh! I am longing thee to see! "
But the headsman was as stolid as the rock,
And the axe fell heavily on the block,
And the scaffold did shake with the terrible shock,
As the body of noble Wallace fell,
Who had fought for Scotland so well.

LINES IN PRAISE OF TOMMY ATKINS

Success to Tommy Atkins, he's a very brave man,
And to deny it there's few people can ;
And to face his foreign foes he's never afraid,
Therefore he's not a beggar, as Rudyard Kipling has said.

No, he's paid by our Government, and is worthy of his hire;
And from our shores in time of war he makes our foes retire,
He doesn't need to beg ; no, nothing so low ;
No, he considers it more honourable to face a foreign foe.

No, he's not a beggar, he's a more useful man,
And, as Shakespeare has said, his life's but a span ;
And at the cannon's mouth he seeks for reputation,
He doesn't go from door to door seeking a donation.

Oh, think of Tommy Atkins when from home far away,
Lying on the battlefield, earth's cold clay ;
And a stone or his knapsack pillowing his head,
And his comrades lying near by him wounded and dead.

And while lying there, poor fellow, he thinks of his wife at
    home,
And his heart bleeds at the thought, and he does moan ;
And down his cheek flows many a silent tear,
When he thinks of his friends and children dear.

Kind Christians, think of him when far, far away,
Fighting for his Queen and Country without dismay ;
May God protect him wherever he goes,
And give him strength to conquer his foes.

To call a soldier a beggar is a very degrading name,
And in my opinion it's a very great shame ;
And the man that calls him a beggar is not the soldier's
    friend,
And no sensible soldier should on him depend.

A soldier is a man that ought to be respected,
And by his country shouldn't be neglected ;
For he fights our foreign foes, and in danger of his life,
Leaving behind him his relatives and his dear wife.

Then hurrah for Tommy Atkins, he's the people's friend,
Because when foreign foes assail us he does us defend ;
He is not a beggar, as Rudyard Kipling has said,
No, he doesn't need to beg, he lives by his trade.

And in conclusion I will say,
Don't forget his wife and children when he's far away ;
But try and help them all you can,
For remember Tommy Atkins is a very useful man.

THE RELIEF OF MAFEKING

Success to Colonel Baden-Powell and his praises loudly
    sing,
For being so brave in relieving Mafeking,
With his gallant little band of eight hundred men,
They made the Boers fly from Mafeking like sheep escaping
    from a pen.

'Twas in the year of 1900 and on the 18th of May,
That Colonel Baden-Powell beat the Boers without dismay,
And made them fly from Mafeking without delay,
Which will be handed down to posterity for many a day.

Colonel Baden-Powell is a very brave man,
And to deny it, I venture to say, few men can ;
He is a noble hero be it said,
For at the siege of Mafeking he never was afraid.

And during the siege Colonel Baden was cheerful and gay,
While the starving population were living on brawn each
    day ;
And alas! the sufferings of the women and children were
    great,
Yet they all submitted patiently to their fate.

For seven months besieged they fought the Boers without
    dismay,
Until at last the Boers were glad to run away ;
Because Baden-Powell's gallant band put them to flight
By cannon shot and volleys of musketry to the left and
    right.

Then long live Baden-Powell and his brave little band,
For during the siege of Mafeking they made a bold stand
Against yelling thousands of Boers who were thirsting for
    their blood,
But as firm as a rock against them they fearlessly stood.

Oh! think of them living on brawn extracted from horse
   hides,
While the inhuman Boers their sufferings deride,
Knowing that the women's hearts with grief were torn
As they looked on their children's faces that looked sad and
   forlorn.

For 217 days the Boers tried to obtain Mafeking's surrender,
But their strategy was futile owing to its noble defender,
Colonel Baden-Powell, that hero of renown,
Who, by his masterly generalship, saved the town.

Methinks I see him and his gallant band,
Looking terror to the foe : Oh! The sight was really grand,
As he cried, " Give it them, lads ; let's do or die ;
And from Mafeking we'll soon make them fly,
And we'll make them rue their rash undertaking
The day they laid siege to the town of Mafeking."

Long life and prosperity to Colonel Baden-Powell,
For there's very few generals can him excel ;
And he is now the Hero of Mafeking, be it told,
And his name should be engraved on medals of gold.

I wish him and his gallant little band every success,
For relieving the people of Mafeking while in distress ;
They made the Boers rue their rash undertaking
The day they laid siege to the town of Mafeking.

For during the defence of Mafeking
From grief he kept the people's hearts from breaking,
Because he sang to them and did recite
Passages from Shakespeare which did their hearts delight.

THE BATTLE OF GLENCOE

Twas in the month of October, and in the year of 1899,
Which the Boers will remember for a very long time,
Because by the British Army they received a crushing blow ;
And were driven from Smith's Hill at the Battle of Glencoe.

The Boers' plan of the battle was devised with great skill,
And about 7000 men of them were camped on Smith's Hill;
And at half-past five the battle began,
And the Boers behaved bravely to a man.

At twenty minutes to six two of the British batteries opened
    fire,
And early in the fight some of the Boers began to retire ;
And in half an hour the Boers' artillery had ceased to fire,
And from the crest of the hill they began to retire.

And General Symons with his staff was watching every detail,
The brave hero whose courage in the battle didn't fail ;
Because he ordered the King's Royal Rifles and the Dublin
    Fusiliers,
To advance in skirmishing order, which they did with three
    cheers.

Then they boldly advanced in very grand style,
And encouraged by their leaders all the while ;
And their marching in skirmishing order was beautiful to see,
As they advanced boldly to attack the enemy.

For over an hour the advance continued without dismay,
Until they had to take a breath by the way ;
They felt so fatigued climbing up Smith's Hill,
But, nevertheless, the brave heroes did it with a will.

They they prepared to attack the enemy,
And with wild battle-cries they attacked them vigorously ;
And with one determined rush they ascended the hill,
And drove the Boers from their position sore against their
    will.

But, alas, General Symons received a mortal wound,
Which caused his soldiers' sorrow to be profound ;
But still they fought on manfully without any dread ;
But, alas, brave General Symons now is dead.

Oh! It was a most inspiring and a magnificent sight,
To see the Hussars spurring their steeds with all their might ;
And charging the Boers with their lances of steel,
Which hurled them from their saddles and made them reel.

The battle raged for six hours and more,
While British cannon Smith's Hill up tore ;
Still the Boers fought manfully, without dismay,
But in a short time they had to give way.

For the Gordon Highlanders soon put an end to the fight,
Oh! it was a most gorgeous and thrilling sight,
To see them with their bagpipes playing, and one ringing
    cheer,
And from Smith's Hill they soon did the Boers clear.

And at the charge of the bayonet they made them fly,
While their leaders cried, " Forward, my lads, do or die ",
And the Boers' blood copiously they did spill,
And the Boers were forced to fly from Smith's Hill.

And in conclusion I hope and pray
The British will be successful when from home far away ;
And long may the Gordons be able to conquer the foe,
At home or abroad, wherever they go.

THE CAPTURE OF HAVANA

'Twas in the year 1762 that France and Spain
Resolved, allied together, to crush Britain ;
But the British Army sailed from England in May,
And arrived off Havana without any delay.

And the British Army resolved to operate on land,
And the appearance of the British troops were really grand
And by the Earl of Albemarle the British troops wer
    commanded,
All eager for to fight as soon as they were landed.

Arduous and trying was the work the British had to do,
Yet with a hearty goodwill they to it flew ;
While the tropical sun on them blazed down,
But the poor soldiers wrought hard and didn't frown.

The bombardment was opened on the 30th of June,
And from the British battleships a fierce cannonade did
  boom ;
And continued from six in the morning till two o'clock in
  the afternoon,
And with grief the French and Spaniards sullenly did
  gloom.

And by the 26th of July the guns of Fort Moro were
  destroyed,
And the French and Spaniards were greatly annoyed ;
Because the British troops entered the Fort without dismay,
And drove them from it at the bayonet charge without
  delay.

But for the safety of the city the Governor organised a night
  attack,
Thinking to repulse the British and drive them back;
And with fifteen hundred militia he did the British attack,
But the British trench guards soon drove them back.

Then the Spandiards were charged and driven down the
  hill,
At the point of the bayonet sore against their will ;
And they rushed to their boats, the only refuge they could
  find,
Leaving a trail of dead and wounded behind.

Then Lieutenant Forbes, at the head of his men,
Swept round the ramparts driving all before them ;
And with levelled bayonets they drove them to and fro,
Then the British flag was hoisted over the bastions of
  Moro.

Then the Governor of the castle fell fighting sword in hand,
While rallying his men around the flagstaff the scene was
  grand ;
And the Spaniards fought hard to save their ships of war,
But the British destroyed their ships and scattered them
  afar.

And every man in the Moro Fort was bayonet or shot,
Which in Spanish history will never be forgot ;
And on the 10th of August Lord Albemarle sent a flag of
  truce,
And summoned the Governor to surrender, but he seemed to
  refuse.

Then from the batteries the British opened a terrific fire,
And the Spaniards from their guns were forced to retire,
Because no longer could they the city defend ;
Then the firing ceased and hostilities were at an end.

Then the city of Havana surrendered unconditionally,
And terms were settled, and the harbour, forts, and city,
With a district of one hundred miles to the westward,
And loads of gold and silver were the British troops' reward.

And all other valuable property was brought to London,
The spoils that the British Army had won ;
And it was conveyed in grand procession to the Tower of
  London,
And the Londoners applauded the British for the honours
  they had won.

THE BATTLE OF WATERLOO

'Twas in the year 1815, and on the 18th day of June,
That British cannon, against the French army, loudly did
    boom,
Upon the ever memorable bloody field of Waterloo ;
Which Napoleon remembered while in St. Helena, and
    bitterly did rue.

The morning of the 18th was gloomy and cheerless to behold,
But the British soon recovered from the severe cold
That they had endured the previous rainy night ;
And each man prepared to burnish his arms for the coming
    fight.

Then the morning passed in mutual arrangements for battle,
And the French guns, at half-past eleven, loudly did rattle ;
And immediately the order for attack was given,
Then the bullets flew like lightning till the Heaven's seemed
    riven.

The place from which Bonaparte viewed the bloody field
Was the farmhouse of La Belle Alliance, which some pro-
    tection did yield ;
And there he remained for the most part of the day,
Pacing to and fro with his hands behind him in doubtful
    dismay.

The Duke of Wellington stood upon a bridge behind La Haye,
And viewed the British army in all their grand array,
And where danger threatened most the noble Duke was
    found
In the midst of shot and shell on every side around.

Hougemont was the key of the Duke of Wellington's position,
A spot that was naturally very strong, and a great acqusition
To the Duke and his staff during the day,
Which the Coldstream Guards held to the last, without
dismay.

The French 2nd Corps were principally directed during the
day
To carry Hougemont farmhouse without delay ;
So the farmhouse in quick succession they did attack,
But the British guns on the heights above soon drove them
back.

But still the heavy shot and shells ploughed through the
walls ;
Yet the brave Guards resolved to hold the place no matter
what befalls ;
And they fought manfully to the last, with courage un-
shaken,
Until the tower of Hougemont was in a blaze but still it
remained untaken.

By these desperate attacks Napoleon lost ten thousand men,
And left them weltering in their gore like sheep in a pen ;
And the British lost one thousand men—which wasn't very
great,
Because the great Napoleon met with a crushing defeat.

The advance of Napoleon on the right was really very fine,
Which was followed by a general onset upon the British line,
In which three hundred pieces of artillery opened their
cannonade ;
But the British artillery played upon them, and great
courage displayed.

For ten long hours it was a continued succession of attacks ;
Whilst the British cavalry charged them in all their draw-
backs ;
And the courage of the British Army was great in square at
Waterloo,
Because hour after hour they were mowed down in numbers
not a few.

At times the temper of the troops had very nearly failed,
Especially amongst the Irish regiments who angry railed ;
And they cried : " When will we get at them ? Show us the
way
That we may avenge the death of our comrades without
delay ? "

" But be steady and cool, my brave lads," was their officers'
command,
While each man was ready to charge with gun in hand ;
Oh, Heaven! it was pitiful to see their comrades lying
around,
Dead and weltering in their gore, and cumbering the
ground.

It was a most dreadful sight to behold,
Heaps upon heaps of dead men lying stiff and cold ;
While the cries of the dying was lamentable to hear ;
And for the loss of their comrades many a soldier shed
a tear.

Men and horses fell on every side around,
Whilst heavy cannon shot tore up the ground ;
And musket balls in thousands flew,
And innocent blood bedewed the field of Waterloo.

Methinks I see the solid British square,
Whilst the shout of the French did rend the air,
As they rush against the square of steel.
Which forced them back and made them reel.

And when a gap was made in that square,
The cry of " Close up! Close up! " did rend the air,
" And charge them with your bayonets, and make them fly!
And Scotland for ever! be the cry."

The French and British closed in solid square,
While the smoke of the heavy cannonade darkened the air ;
Then the noble Picton deployed his division into line,
And drove back the enemy in a very short time.

Then Lord Anglesey seized on the moment, and charging
    with the Greys,
Whilst the Inniskillings burst through everything, which
    they did always ;
Then the French infantry fell in hundreds by the swords of
    the Dragoons ;
Whilst the thundering of the cannonade loudly booms.

And the Eagles of the 45th and 105th were all captured that
    day,
And upwards of 2000 prisoners, all in grand array ;
But, alas! at the head of his division, the noble Picton fell,
While the Highlanders played a lament for him they loved
    so well.

Then the French cavalry receded from the square they
    couldn't penetrate,
Still Napoleon thought to weary the British into defeat ;
But when he saw his columns driven back in dismay,
He cried, " How beautifully these English fight, but they
    must give way."

And well did British bravery deserve the proud encomium,
Which their enduring courage drew from the brave Napoleon;
And when the close column of infantry came on the British
square,
Then the British gave one loud cheer which did rend the air.

Then the French army pressed forward at Napoleon's
command,
Determined, no doubt, to make a bold stand ;
Then Wellington cried, " Up Guards and break their ranks
through,
And chase the French invaders from off the field of Waterloo! "

Then, in a moment, they were all on their feet,
And they met the French, sword in hand, and made them
retreat ;
Then Wellington in person directed the attack,
And at every point and turning the French were beaten
back.

And the road was choked and encumbered with the dead ;
And, unable to stand the charge, the French instantly fled,
And Napoleon's army of yesterday was now a total wreck,
Which the British manfully for ten long hours held in check.

Then, panic-struck, the French were forced to yield,
And Napoleon turned his charger's head, and fled from the
field,
With his heart full of woe, no doubt—
Exclaiming, " Oh, Heaven! my noble army has met with a
total rout! "

THE ALBION BATTLESHIP CALAMITY

'Twas in the year of 1898, and on the 21st of June,
The launching of the Battleship Albion caused a great
   gloom,
Amongst the relatives of many persons who were drowned
   in the River Thames,
Which their relatives will remember while life remains.

The vessel was christened by the Duchess of York,
And the spectators' hearts felt as light as cork
As the Duchess cut the cord that was holding the fine ship,
Then the spectators loudly cheered as the vessel slid down
   the slip.

The launching of the vessel was very well carried out,
While the guests on the stands cheered without any
   doubt,
Under the impression that everything would go well ;
But, alas ! instantaneously a bridge and staging fell.

Oh ! little did the Duchess of York think that day
That so many lives would be taken away
At the launching of the good ship Albion,
But when she heard of the catastrophe she felt woebegone.

But accidents will happen without any doubt,
And often the cause thereof is hard to find out ;
And according to report, I've heard people say,
'Twas the great crowd on the bridge caused it to give
   way.

Just as the vessel entered the water the bridge and staging
  gave way,
Immersing some three hundred people which caused great
  dismay
Amongst thousands of spectators that were standing there,
And in the faces of the bystanders were depicted despair.

Then the police boats instantly made for the fatal spot,
And with the aid of dockyard hands several people were
  got,
While some scrambled out themselves, the best way they
  could—
And the most of them were the inhabitants of the neighbour-
  hood.

Part of them were the wives and daughters of the dockyard
  hands,
And as they gazed upon them they in amazement
  stands ;
And several bodies were hauled up quite dead,
Which filled the onlookers' hearts with pity and dread.

One of the first rescued was a little baby,
Which was conveyed away to a mortuary ;
And several were taken to the fitter's shed, and attended to
  there
By the firemen and several nurses with the greatest care.

Meanwhile heartrending scenes were taking place,
Whilst the tears ran down many a Mother and Father's
  face,
That had lost their children in the River Thames,
Which they will remember while life remains.

Oh, Heaven! it was horrible to see the bodies laid out
in rows,
And as Fathers and Mothers passed along, adown their
cheeks the tears flows,
While their poor, sickly hearts were throbbing with fear.

A great crowd had gathered to search for the missing
dead,
And many strong men broke down because their heart with
pity bled,
As they looked upon the distorted faces of their relatives
dear,
While adown their cheeks flowed many a silent tear.

The tenderest sympathy, no doubt, was shown to them,
By the kind hearted Police and Firemen ;
The scene in fact was most sickening to behold,
And enough to make one's blood run cold,
To see tear-stained men and women there
Searching for their relatives, and in their eyes a pitiful
stare.

There's one brave man in particular I must mention,
And I'm sure he's worthy of the people's attention :
His name is Thomas Cooke, of No. 6 Percy Road, Canning
Town,
Who's name ought to be to posterity handed down,
Because he leapt into the River Thames, and heroically did
behave,
And rescued five persons from a watery grave.

Mr Wilson, a young Electrician, got a terrible fright,
When he saw his mother and sister dead—he was shocked at
the sight,
Because his sister had not many days returned from her
honeymoon,
And in his countenance, alas! there was a sad gloom.

Her Majesty has sent a message of sympathy to the bereaved
ones in distress,
And the Duke and Duchess of York have sent 25 guineas I
must confess,
And £1000 from the Directors of the Thames Ironworks and
Shipbuilding Company,
Which I hope will help to fill the bereaved one's hearts with
glee.

And in conclusion I will venture to say,
That accidents will happen by night and by day ;
And I will say without any fear,
Because to me it appears quite clear,
That the stronger we our houses do build,
The less chance we have of being killed.

AN ALL NIGHT SEA FIGHT

Ye sons of Mars, come list to me,
And I will relate to ye
A great and heroic naval fight,
Which will fill your hearts with delight.

The fight was between the French Frigate " Pique " and the
   British Frigate " Blanche,"
But the British crew were bold and staunch ;
And the battle was fought in West Indian waters in the year
   of 1795,
And for to gain the victory the French did nobly strive.

And on the morning of the 4th of January while cruising off
   Gadulope,
The look-out man from the foretop loudly spoke,
And cried, " Sail ahoy ! " " Where away ? "
" On the lee bow, close in shore, sir," was answered without
   delay.

Then Captain Faulkner cried, " Clear the decks ! "
And the French vessel with his eyeglass he inspects ;
And he told his men to hoist the British flag,
And " prepare my heroes to pull down that French rag."

Then the "Blanche" made sail and bore away
In the direction of the "Pique" without delay ;
And Captain Faulkner cried, " Now, my lads, bear down on
   him,
And make ready quickly and begin."

It was about midnight when the Frenchman hove in sight,
And could be seen distinctly in the starlight ;
And for an hour and a half they fired away
Broadsides into each other without dismay.

And with tne rapid flashes the Heavens were aflame,
As each volley from the roaring cannons came ;
And the incessant roll of musketry was awful to hear,
As it broke over the silent sea and smote upon the ear.

130

The French vessel had nearly 400 men,
Her decks were literally crowded from stem to stern ;
And the musketeers kept up a fierce fire on the " Blanche,"
But still the "Blanche" on them did advance.

And the "Blanche's" crew without dismay
Fired a broadside into the "Pique" without delay,
Which raked her fore and aft, and knocked her to smash,
And the mizenmast fell overboard with a terrible crash.

Then the Frenchmen rushed forward to board the
    " Blanche,"
But in doing so they had a very poor chance,
For the British Tars in courage didn't lack,
Because thrice in succession on their own deck they were
    driven back.

Then "Bravo, my lads!" Captain Faulkner loudly cries,
"Lash her bowsprit to our capstan, she's our prize" ;
And he seized some ropes to lash round his foe,
But a musket ball pierced his heart and laid him low.

Then a yell of rage burst from the noble crew,
And near to his fallen body they drew ;
And tears for his loss fell fast on the deck,
Their grief was so great their tears they couldn't check.

The crew was very sorry for their captain's downfall,
But the sight didn't their brave hearts appal ;
Because they fastened the ropes to the "Pique" at the
    capstan,
And the " Pique " was dragged after the " Blanche," the
    sight was grand.

Yet the crew of the "Pique" maintained the fight,
Oh! most courageously they fought in the dead of night ;
And for two hours they kept up firing without dismay,
But it was a sacrifice of human life, they had to give way.

And about five o'clock in the morning the French cried for
    quarter,
Because on board there had been a great slaughter ;
Their Captain Cousail was mortally wounded in the fight
Along with many officers and men ; oh! it was a heart-
    rending sight
To see the wounded and dead weltering in their gore
After thecannonading had ceased and the fighting was o'er.

THE WRECK OF THE STEAMER "STELLA"

'Twas in the month of March and in the year of 1899,
Which will be remembered for a very long time ;
The wreck of the steamer "Stella" that was wrecked on the
    Casquet Rocks,
By losing her bearings in a fog, and received some terrible
    shocks.

The "Stella" was bound for the Channel Islands on a holiday
    trip,
And a number of passengers were resolved not to let the
    chance slip ;
And the hearts of the passengers felt light and gay,
As the "Stella" steamed out of the London Docks without
    delay.

The vessel left London at a quarter-past eleven,
With a full passenger list and a favourable wind from
heaven;
And all went well until late in the afternoon,
When all at once a mist arose, alas! too soon.

And as the Channel Islands were approached a fog set in,
Then the passengers began to be afraid and made a chatter-
ing din;
And about half-past three o'clock the fog settled down,
Which caused Captain Reeks and the passengers with fear
to frown.

And brave Captain Reeks felt rather nervous and discontent,
Because to him it soon became quite evident;
And from his long experience he plainly did see
That the fog was increasing in great density.

Still the "Stella" sailed on at a very rapid rate,
And, of, heaven! rushed headlong on to her fate,
And passed o'er the jagged rocks without delay,
And her side was ripped open: Oh! horror and dismay!

Then all the passengers felt the terrible shock,
As the "Stella" stuck fast upon the first ledge of rock;
And they rushed to the deck in wild alarm,
While some of them cried: "Oh! God protect us from
harm."

Then men clasped wives and daughters, and friends shook
hands,
And unmoved Captain Reeks upon the bridge stands;
And he shouted, "Get out the boats without delay!"
Then the sailors and officers began to work without dismay.

Again Captain Reeks cried in a manly clear voice,
" Let the women and children be our first choice! "
Then the boats were loaded in a speedy way,
And with brave seamen to navigate them that felt no
    dismay.

Then the "Stella" began rapidly for to settle down,
And Captain Reeks gave his last order without a frown,
Shouting, "Men, for yourselves, you'll better look out! "
Which they did, needing no second bidding, without fear or
    doubt.

Then the male passengers rushed to the boats in wild
    despair,
While the cries of the women and children rent the air ;
Oh, heaven! such a scene! 'twas enough to make one weep,
To see mothers trying to save their children that were fast
    asleep.

Brave Captain Reeks stood on the bridge till the ship went
    down,
With his eyes uplifted towards heaven, and on his face no
    frown ;
And some of the passengers jumped from the ship into the
    sea,
And tried hard to save their lives right manfully.

But the sufferings of the survivors are pitiful to hear,
And I think all Christian people for them will drop a tear,
Because the rower of the boats were exhausted with damp
    and cold ;
And the heroine of the wreck was Miss Greta Williams, be it
    told.

She remained in an open boat with her fellow-passengers and
    crew,
And sang "O rest in the Lord, and He will come to our
    rescue" ;
And for fourteen hours they were rowing on the mighty
    deep,
And when each man was done with his turn he fell asleep.

And about six o'clock in the morning a man shrieked out,
"There's a sailing boat coming towards us without any
    doubt " ;
And before the sailing boat could get near, a steamer hove
    in sight,
Which proved to be the steamer " Lynx," to their delight.

And they were conveyed to Guernsey without delay,
Poor souls, with their hearts in a state of joy and dismay ;
But alas ! more than eighty persons have been lost in the
    briny deep,
But I hope their souls are now in heaven in safe keep.

THE WRECK OF THE STEAMER
"STORM QUEEN"

Ye landsmen, all pray list to me,
While I relate a terrible tale of the sea,
Concerning the screw steamer "Storm Queen"
Which was wrecked, alas ! a most heart-rending scene.

From Sebastopol, with a cargo of grain, she was on her way,
And soon after entering the Bay of Biscay,
On the 21st of December, they experienced a fearful storm
Such as they never experienced since they were born.

The merciless sea was running mountains high,
And to save themselves from a watery grave manfully they
  did try ;
But the vessel became unmanageable, but still they worked
  away,
And managed to launch two small boats without dismay.

They wrought most manfully and behaved very well,
But a big wave smashed a small boat before they left the
  vessel ;
Still the Captain, Mr Jaques, and five of the crew
Clung to the "Storm Queen" until she sank beneath the
  waters blue.

While the sea lashed itself into white foam and loudly did
  roar,
And with a gurgling sound the big waves covered the vessel
  o'er ;
So perished Captain Jaques and five of the crew
Who stuck to the vessel, as brave sailors would do.

But before the vessel sank a raft was made,
And a few men got on to it who were not afraid ;
And oh! it was enough to make one's blood to freeze
To see them jumping off the steamer into the yawning
  seas.

So they were tossed about on the big billows the whole
    night,
And beneath the big waves they were engulphed before
    daylight ;
But 22 that reached the boats were saved in all
By the aid of God, on whom they did call.

And on the next morning before daylight
The Norwegian barque "Gulvare" hove in sight ;
Then they shouted and pulled towards her with all their
    might,
While the seas were running high, oh ! what a fearful sight.

The poor souls were prevented from getting along side
Of the barque "Gulvare" by the heavy seas and tide ;
And as the boats drew near the barque the storm increases
Until the boats struck against her and were dashed to pieces.

It was almost beyond human efforts with the storm to cope,
But most fortunately they were hauled on board by a rope,
While the big waves did lash the barque all over,
But by a merciful providence they were landed safely at
    Dover.

The survivors when rescued were in a destitute state,
But nevertheless they seemed resigned to their fate,
And they thanked God that did them save
Most timely from a cold and watery grave.

And during their stay in Dover they received kind treatment,
For which they, poor creatures, felt very content ;
And when they recovered from their ills they met at sea,
The authorities sent them home to their own country.

But as for Captain Jaques, few men like him had been,
Because he couldn't be persuaded to desert the "Storm
  Queen,"
As he declared he wouldn't leave her whatever did betide ;
So the brave hero sank with her beneath the waters wide.

THE WRECK OF THE
"ABERCROMBIE ROBINSON"

'Twas in the year of 1842 and on the 27th of May
That six Companies of the 91st Regiment with spirits light
  and gay,
And forming the Second Battalion, left Naas without delay,
Commanded by Captain Bertie Gordon, to proceed to the
  Cape straightaway.

And on the second of June they sailed for the Cape of Good
  Hope
On board the "Abercrombie Robinson," a vessel with which
  few vessels could cope ;
And in August the 25th they reached Table Bay,
Where a battalion of the 91st was warned for service without
  delay.

To relieve the 91st, which was to be stationed at Cape
  Town,
An order which the 91st obeyed without a single frown ;
And all the officers not on duty obtained leave to go
  ashore,
Leaving only six aboard, in grief to deplore.

There were 460 men of the 91st seemingly all content,
Besides a draft of the Cape Mounted Rifles and a draft of
  the 27th Regiment ;
But, alas an hour after midnight on the same night
A strong gale was blowing, which filled the passengers'
  hearts with fright.

The ship pitched heavily and could be felt touching the
  ground,
Then Captain Gordon warned the Sergeant-Major and officers
  all round,
That they might expect a storm, to him it seemed plain;
And, as he predicted, it blew a terrific hurricane.

And the passengers' hearts were filled with dismay,
And a little after three o'clock in the morning the cable
  broke away,
Then the ship drifted helplessly before the merciless storm,
While the women and children looked sad, pale and
  forlorn.

Then the thunder roared and the lightning flashed in bright
  array,
And was one of the greatest storms ever raged over Table
  Bay,
And the ill-fated vessel drove in towards the shore,
While the Storm Fiend did laugh and loudly did **roar.**

And the ship rolled and heaved with the raging tide,
While the seas poured down the hatchways and broke over
  her side,
And the ship wrought for herself a bed in the sand ;
Still Captain Bertie hoped all might get safely to land.

'Twas about seven o'clock when daylight did appear,
And when the storm ceases the passengers gave a cheer,
Who had been kept below during the awful night,
Then in small groups they came on deck, a most pitiful
    sight.

Alas! sad and dejected, sickly looking, pale and forlorn,
Owing to the close confinement during the storm ;
And for a time attempts were made to send a rope
    ashore,
But these proved futile owing to the raging billows which
    loudly did roar.

Then one of the ship's cutters was carefully lowered over
    the side,
And her crew towards the shore merrily did glide,
And succeeded in reaching the shore with a leading line,
And two boats were conveyed to the sinking ship just in
    time.

And to save the women and children from being drowned,
Captain Gordon gave orders to the 91st all round
For the women and children to disembark immediately,
Who to God were crying for help most frantically.

And the 91st made a most determined stand,
While lowering the women and children it was awful and
    grand,
As they lowered them gently into the boats over the ship's
    side,
Regardless of their own lives whatever would betide.

Then the sick were to disembark after the women and
  children,
And next the 27th Regiment and Cape Mounted Riflemen ;
And from half-past eight till ten o'clock the disembarkation
  went on,
While the women and children looked ghastly pale and woe
  begone.

The disembarkation of the 91st came at last,
And as there were only two boats available they stood
  aghast,
Because the boats only carried each time thirty ;
Still, the work went on for four hours most manfully.

And at half-past three the last boat left the ship's side,
And o'er the raging billows the small boats did glide,
Containing the officers and crew who remained to the last,
To see the women and children saved and all danger past.

And after a night of great danger and through a raging sea
Seven hundred souls were carried from a sinking ship provi-
  dentially ;
And among them were trembling children and nervous
  women also,
And sick men who were dying with their hearts full of woe.

But thank God they were all saved and brought to land,
All through Colonel Bertie Gordon, who wisely did com-
  mand
The 91st to see to the women and children's safety,
An order which they obeyed right manfully ;
And all honour is due to the 91st for their gallantry,
Likewise Captain Bertie Gordon, who behaved so heroically.

THE LOSS OF THE "VICTORIA"

Alas ! Now o'er Britannia there hangs a gloom,
Because over 400 British Tars have met with a watery tomb;
Who served aboard the " Victoria," the biggest ship in the
  navy,
And one of the finest battleships that ever sailed the sea.

And commanded by Sir George Tyron, a noble hero bold,
And his name on his tombstone should be written in letters
  of gold ;
For he was skifull in naval tactics, few men could with him
  cope,
And he was considered to be the nation's hope.

'Twas on Thursday, She twenty-second of June,
And off the coast of tyria, and in the afternoon,
And in the year of our Lord eighteen ninety-three,
That the ill-fated "Victoria" sank to the bottom of the sea.

The "Victoria" sank in fifteen minutes after she was rammed,
In eighty fathoms of water, which was smoothly calmed ;
The monster war vessel capsized bottom uppermost,
And, alas, lies buried in the sea totally lost.

The "Victoria" was the flagship of the Mediterranean Fleet,
And was struck by the "Camperdown" when too close they
  did meet,
While practising the naval and useful art of war,
How to wheel and discharge their shot at the enemy
  afar.

Oh, Heaven! Methinks I see some men lying in their beds,
And some skylarking, no doubt, and not a soul dreads
The coming avalanche that was to seal their doom,
Until down came the mighty fabric of the engine room.

Then death leaped on them from all quarters in a moment,
And there were explosions of magazines and boilers rent;
And the fire and steam and water beat out all life,
But I hope the drowned ones are in the better world free from strife.

Sir George Tyron was on the bridge at the moment of the accident
With folded arms, seemingly quite content;
And seeing the vessel couldn't be saved he remained till the last,
And went down with the "Victoria" when all succour was past.

Methinks I see him on the bridge like a hero brave,
And the ship slowly sinking into the briny wave;
And when the men cried, "Save yourselves without delay,"
He told them to save themselves, he felt no dismay.

'Twas only those that leaped from the vessel at the first alarm,
Luckily so, that were saved from any harm
By leaping into the boats o'er the vessel's side,
Thanking God they had escaped as o'er the smooth water they did glide.

At Whitehall, London, mothers and fathers did call,
And the pitiful scene did the spectators' hearts appal;
But the most painful case was the mother of J. P. Scarlet,
Who cried, "Oh, Heaven, the loss of my son I'll never
  forget."

Oh, Heaven! Befriend the bereaved ones, hard is their fate,
Which I am sorry at heart to relate;
But I hope God in His goodness will provide for them,
Especially the widows, for the loss of their men.

Alas! Britannia now will mourn the loss of her naval com-
  mander,
Who was as brave as the great Alexander;
And to his honour be it fearlessly told,
Few men would excel this hero bold.

Alas! 'Tis sad to be buried in eighty fathoms of Syrian sea,
Which will hide the secret of the "Victoria" to all eternity;
Which causes Britannia's sorrow to be profound
For the brave British Tars that have been drowned.

THE BURNING OF THE SHIP "KENT"

Good people of high and low degree,
I pray ye all to list to me,
And I'll relate a harrowing tale of the sea
Concerning the burning of the ship "Kent" in the Bay of
  Biscay,
Which is the most appalling tale of the present century.

She carried a crew, including officers, of 148 men,
And twenty lady passengers along with them ;
Besides 344 men of the 31st Regiment,
And twenty officers with them, all seemingly content.

Also the soldiers' wives, which numbered forty-three,
And sixty-six children, a most beautiful sight to see ;
And in the year of 1825, and on the 19th of February,
The ship "Kent" sailed from the Downs right speedily,
While the passengers' hearts felt light with glee.

And the beautiful ship proceeded on her way to Bengal,
While the passengers were cheerful one and all ;
And the sun shone out in brilliant array,
And on the evening of the 28th they entered the Bay of
   Biscay.

But a gale from the south-west sprang up that night,
Which filled the passengers' hearts with fright ;
And it continued to increase in violence as the night wore on,
Whilst the lady passengers looked very woe-begone.

Part of the cargo in the hold consisted of shot and shell,
And the vessel rolled heavily as the big billows rose and fell ;
Then two sailors descended the forehold carrying a light,
To see if all below was safe and right.

And they discovered a spirit cask and the contents oozing
   rapidly,
And the man with the light stooped to examine it immediately ;
And in doing so he dropped the lamp while in a state of
   amaze,
And, oh horror! in a minute the forehold was in a blaze.

It was two o'clock in the morning when the accident took
    place,
And, alas! horror and fear was depicted in each face ;
And the sailors tried hard to extinguish the flame,
But, oh Heaven! all their exertions proved in vain.

The inflammable matter rendered their efforts of no avail,
And the brave sailors with over-exertion looked very pale ;
And for hours in the darkness they tried to check the fire,
But the flames still mounted higher and higher.

But Captain Cobb resolved on a last desperate experiment,
Because he saw the ship was doomed, and he felt discontent ;
Then he raised the alarm that the ship was on fire,
Then the passengers quickly from their beds did retire.

And women and children rushed to the deck in wild despair,
And, paralysed with terror, many women tore their hair ;
And some prayed to God for help, and wildly did screech,
But, alas! poor souls, help was not within their reach.

Still the gale blew hard, and the waves ran mountains high,
While men, women, and children bitterly did cry
To God to save them from the merciless fire ;
But the flames rose higher and higher.

And when the passengers had lost all hope, and in great
    dismay,
The look-out man shouted, " Ho! a sail coming this way ";
Then every heart felt light and gay,
And signals of distress were hoisted without delay.

Then the vessel came to their rescue, commanded by Captain
  Cook,
And he gazed upon the burning ship with a pitiful look ;
She proved to be the brig " Cambria," bound for Vera Cruz,
Then the captain cried, " Men, save all ye can, there's no
  time to lose."

Then the sailors of the "Cambria" wrought with might and
  main,
While the sea spray fell on them like heavy rain ;
First the women and children were transferred from the
  "Kent"
By boats, ropes, and tackle without a single accident.

But, alas ! the fire had reached the powder magazine,
Then followed an explosion, oh! what a fearful scene ;
But the explosion was witnessed by Captain Babby of the
  ship "Carline,"
Who most fortunately arrived in the nick of time.

And fourteen additional human beings were saved from the
  " Kent,"
And they thanked Captain Babby and God, who to them
  succour sent,
And had saved them from being burnt, and drowned in the
  briny deep ;
And they felt so overjoyed that some of them did weep ;
And in the first port in England they landed without delay,
And when their feet touched English soil their hearts felt
  gay.

THE WRECK OF THE "INDIAN CHIEF"

'Twas on the 8th of January 1881,
That a terrific gale along the English Channel ran,
And spread death and disaster in its train,
Whereby the "Indian Chief" vessel was tossed on the raging
    main.

She was driven ashore on the Goodwin Sands,
And the good captain fearlessly issued his commands,
" Come, my men, try and save the vessel, work with all your
    might,"
Although the poor sailors on board were in a fearful plight.

They were expecting every minute her hull would give way,
And they, poor souls, felt stricken with dismay,
And the captain and some of the crew clung to the main
    masts,
Where they were exposed to the wind's cold blasts.

A fierce gale was blowing and the sea ran mountains high,
And the sailors on board heaved many a bitter sigh ;
And in the teeth of the storm the lifeboat was rowed bravely
Towards the ship in distress, which was awful to see.

The ship was lifted high on the crest of a wave,
While the sailors tried hard their lives to save,
And implored God to save them from a watery grave,
And through fear some of them began to rave.

The waves were miles long in length,
And the sailors had lost nearly all their strength,
By striving hard their lives to save,
From being drowned in the briny wave.

A ration of rum and a biscuit was served out to each man,
And the weary night passed, and then appeared the morning
  dawn ;
And when the lifeboat hove in sight a sailor did shout,
" Thank God, there's she at last without any doubt."

But, with weakness and the biting cold,
Several of the sailors let go their hold ;
And, alas, fell into the yawning sea,
Poor souls! and were launched into eternity.

Oh, it was a most fearful plight,
For the poor sailors to be in the rigging all night ;
While the storm fiend did laugh and roar,
And the big waves lashed the ship all o'er.

And as the lifeboat drew near,
The poor sailors raised a faint cheer ;
And all the lifeboat men saw was a solitary mast,
And some sailors clinging to it, while the ship was sinking
  fast.

Charles Tait, the coxswain of the lifeboat, was a skilful
  boatman,
And the bravery he and his crew displayed was really grand ;
For his men were hardy and a very heroic set,
And for bravery their equals it would be hard to get.

But, thank God, out of twenty-nine eleven were saved,
Owing to the way the lifeboat men behaved ;
And when they landed with the eleven wreckers at Rams-
  gate,
The people's joy was very great.

CAPTAIN TEACH *alias* BLACK BEARD

Edward Teach was a native of Bristol, and sailed from that port
On board a privateer, in search of sport,
As one of the crew, during the French War in that station,
And for personal courage he soon gained his Captain's approbation.

'Twas in the spring of 1717, Captain Harnigold and Teach sailed from Providence
For the continent of America, and no further hence ;
And in their way captured a vessel laden with flour,
Which they put on board their own vessels in the space of an hour.

They also seized two other vessels and took some gallons of wine,
Besides plunder to a considerable value, and most of it most costly design ;
And after that they made a prize of a large French Guinea-man,
Then to act an independent part Teach now began.

But the news spread throughout America, far and near,
And filled many of the inhabitants' hearts with fear ;
But Lieutenant Maynard with his sloops of war directly steered,
And left James River on the 17th November in quest of Black Beard,
And on the evening of the 21st came in sight of the pirate ;
And when Black Beard spied his sloops he felt elate.

When he saw the sloops sent to apprehend him,
He didn't lose his courage, but fiendishly did grin;
And told his men to cease from drinking and their tittle-
tattle,
Although he had only twenty men on board, and prepare for
battle.

In case anything should happen to him during the engage-
ment,
One of his men asked him, who felt rather discontent,
Whether his wife knew where he had buried his pelf,
When he impiously replied that nobody knew but the devil
and himself.

In the Morning Maynard weighed and sent his boat to sound,
Which, coming near the pirate, unfortunately ran aground;
But Maynard lightened his vessel of the ballast and water,
Whilst from the pirates' ship small shot loudly did clatter.

But the pirates' small shot or slugs didn't Maynard appal,
He told his men to take their cutlasses and be ready upon
his call;
And to conceal themselves every man below,
While he would remain at the helm and face the foe.

Then Black Beard cried, " They're all knocked on the head,"
When he saw no hands upon deck he thought they were
dead;
Then Black Beard boarded Maynard's sloop without dismay,
But Maynard's men rushed upon deck, then began the
deadly fray.

Then Black Beard and Maynard engaged sword in hand,
And the pirate fought manfully and made a bold stand ;
And Maynard with twelve men, and Black Beard with
    fourteen,
Made the most desperate and bloody conflict that ever was
    seen.

At last with shots and wounds the pirate fell down dead,
Then from his body Maynard severed the pirate's head,
And suspended it upon his bowsprit-end,
And thanked God Who so mercifully did him defend.

Black Beard derived his name from his long black beard,
Which terrified America more than any comet that had ever
    appeared ;
But, thanks be to God, in this age we need not be afeared,
Of any such pirates as the inhuman Black Beard.

THE DISASTROUS FIRE AT SCARBOROUGH

Twas in the year of 1898, and on the 8th of June,
A mother and six children met with a cruel doom
In one of the most fearful fires for some years past—
And as the spectators gazed upon them they stood aghast.

The fire broke out in a hairdresser's, in the town of Scarborough,
And as the fire spread it filled the people's hearts with sorrow ;
But the police and the fire brigade were soon on the ground,
Then the hose and reel were quickly sent round.

Oh! it was horrible to see the flames leaping up all around,
While amongst the spectators the silence was profound,
As they saw a man climb out to the parapet high,
Resolved to save his life, or in the attempt to die!

And he gave one half frantic leap, with his heart full of woe,
And came down upon the roof of a public-house 20 feet below ;
But, alas! he slipped and fell through the skylight,
And received cuts and bruises : oh, what a horrible sight!

He was the tenant of the premises, Mr Brookes,
And for his wife and family he enquires, with anxious looks,
But no one could tell him, it did appear,
And when told so adown his cheeks flowed many a tear.

He had been sleeping by himself on the second floor,
When suddenly alarmed, he thought he'd make sure,
And try to escape from the burning pile with his life,
And try and save his family and his wife.

The fire brigade played on the first floor with great speed,
But the flames had very inflammable fuel upon which to
feed,
So that the fire spread with awful rapidity,
And in twenty minutes the building was doomed to the
fourth storey.

The firemen wrought with might and main,
But still the fire did on them gain,
That it was two hours before they could reach the second
floor,
The heat being so intense they could scarcely it endure.

And inside all the time a woman and six children were there,
And when the firemen saw them, in amazement they did
stare ;
The sight that met their eyes made them for to start—
Oh, Heaven! the sight was sufficient to rend the strongest
heart.

For there was Mrs Brookes stretched dead on the floor,
Who had fallen in trying her escape for to procure.
She was lying with one arm over her ten months old child,
And her cries for help, no doubt, were frantic and wild ;
And part of her arm was burned off as it lay above
The child she was trying to shield, which shows a mother's
love.

For the baby's flesh was partly uninjured by the flames,
Which shows that the loving mother had endured great
pains ;
It, however, met its death by suffocation,
And as the spectators gazed thereon, it filled their hearts
with consternation.

The firemen acted heroically, without any dread,
And when they entered the back premises they found the
  six children dead ;
But Mr Brookes, 'tis said, is still alive,
And I hope for many years he will survive.

Oh, Heaven! it is cruel to perish by fire,
Therefore let us be watchful before to our beds we retire,
And see that everything is in safe order before we fall asleep,
And pray that God o'er us in the night watch will keep.

THE BURIAL OF MR. GLADSTONE

THE GREAT POLITICAL HERO

Alas! the people now do sigh and moan
For the loss of Wm. Ewart Gladstone,
Who was a very great politician and a moral man,
And to gainsay it there's few people can.

'Twas in the year of 1898, and on the 19th of May,
When his soul took its flight for ever and aye,
And his body lies interred in Westminster Abbey ;
But I hope his soul has gone to that Heavenly shore,
Where all trials and troubles cease for evermore.

He was a man of great intellect and genius bright,
And ever faithful to his Queen by day and by night,
And always foremost in a political fight ;
And for his services to mankind, God will him requite.

The funeral procession was affecting to see,
Thousands of people were assembled there, of every degree ;
And it was almost eleven o'clock when the procession left
    Westminster Hall,
And the friends of the deceased were present—physicians
    and all.

A large force of police was also present there,
And in the faces of the spectators there was a pitiful air,
Yet they were orderly in every way,
And newspaper boys were selling publications without delay.

Present in the procession was Lord Playfair,
And Bailie Walcot was also there,
Also Mr Macpherson of Edinboro—
And all seemingly to be in profound sorrow.

The supporters of the coffin were the Earl Rosebery,
And the Right Honourable Earl of Kimberley,
And the Right Honourable Sir W. Vernon he was there,
And His Royal Highness the Duke of York, I do declare.

George Armitstead, Esq., was there also,
And Lord Rendal, with his heart full of woe ;
And the Right Honourable Duke of Rutland,
And the Right Honourable Arthur J. Balfour, on the right
    hand ;
Likewise the noble Marquis of Salisbury,
And His Royal Highness the Prince of Wales, of high degree.

And immediately behind the coffin was Lord Pembroke,
The representative of Her Majesty, and the Duke of Norfolk,
Carrying aloft a beautiful short wand,
The insignia of his high, courtly office, which looked very
    grand.

And when the procession arrived at the grave, Mrs Gladstone was there,
And in her countenance was depicted a very grave air ;
And the dear, good lady seemed to sigh and moan
For her departed, loving husband, Wm. Ewart Gladstone.

And on the opposite side of her stood Lord Pembroke,
And Lord Salisbury, who wore a skull cap and cloak ;
Also the Prince of Wales and the Duke of Rutland,
And Mr Balfour and Lord Spencer, all looking very bland.

And the clergy were gathered about the head of the grave,
And the attention of the spectators the Dean did crave ;
Then he said, " Man that is born of woman hath a short time to live,
But, Oh, Heavenly Father! do thou our sins forgive."

Then Mrs Gladstone and her two sons knelt down by the grave,
Then the Dean did the Lord's blessing crave,
While Mrs Gladstone and her sons knelt,
While the spectators for them great pity felt.

The scene was very touching and profound,
To see all the mourners bending their heads to the ground,
And, after a minute's most silent prayer,
The leave-taking at the grave was affecting, I do declare.

Then Mrs Gladstone called on little Dorothy Drew,
And immediately the little girl to her grandmamma flew,
And they both left the grave with their heads bowed down,
While tears from their relatives fell to the ground.

Immortal Wm. Ewart Gladstone! I must conclude my muse,
And to write in praise of thee my pen does not refuse—
To tell the world, fearlessly, without the least dismay,
You were the greatest politician in your day.

THE DEATH OF THE REV. DR. WILSON

'Twas in the year of 1888 and on the 17th of January
That the late Rev. Dr. Wilson's soul fled away ;
The generous-hearted Dr. had been ailing for some time,
But death, with his dart, did pierce the heart of the learned
   divine.

He was a man of open countenance and of great ability,
And late minister of Free St. Paul's Church, Dundee,
And during the twenty-nine years he remained as minister
   in Dundee
He struggled hard for the well-being of the community.

He was the author of several works concerning great
   men,
In particular the Memoirs of Dr. Candlish and Christ turning
   His face towards Jerusalem ;
Which is well worthy of perusal, I'm sure,
Because the style is concise and the thoughts clear and
   pure.

And as for his age, he was in his eightieth year,
And has left a family of one son and five daughters dear,
And for his loss they will shed many a tear,
Because in their hearts they loved him most dear.

He was a man of a very kindly turn,
And many of his old members for him will mourn,
Because as a preacher he was possessed of courage bold,
Just like one of Covenanting heroes of old.

But I hope he is landed safe on Canaan's bright shore,
To sing with bright angels for evermore
Around that golden throne where God's family doth meet
To sing songs night and day, most sacred and sweet.

The coffin containing the remains was brought on Tuesday
  evening from Edinboro,
And as the relatives witnessed its departure their hearts
  were full of sorrow,
And the remains were laid inside Free St. Paul's Church,
  Dundee,
And interred on Wednesday in the Western Cemetery.

The funeral service began at half-past one o'clock in the
  afternoon,
And with people the church was filled very soon,
And the coffin was placed in the centre of the platform,
And the lid was covered with wreaths which did the coffin
  adorn.

There were beautiful wreaths from the grandchildren of the
  deceased,
Whom I hope is now from all troubles released
Also there were wreaths from Mrs and Miss Young, Windsor
  Street, Dundee,
Which certainly were most beautiful to see.

Besides the tributes of Miss Morrison and Miss H. Morrison
  were a beautiful sight,
Also the tributes of Miss Strong and Mr I. Martin White,
Also Mrs and the Misses Henderson's, West Park, Dundee,
Besides the Misses White Springrove were magnificent
  to see.

The members and office-bearers of the church filled the pews
    on the right,
Which was a very impressive and solemn sight ;
And psalms and hymns were sung by the congregation,
And the Rev. W. I. Cox concluded the service with great
    veneration.

Then the coffin was carried from the church and placed in
    the hearse,
While the congregation allowed the friends to disperse,
Then followed the congregation without delay,
Some to join the procession, while others went home
    straightaway.

The procession consisted of the hearse and 47 carriages no
    less,
Which were drawn up in the Nethergate, I do confess,
And as the cortege passed slowly along the Nethergate,
Large crowds watched the procession and ungrudgingly did
    wait.

And when the hearse reached the cemetery the Rev. R.
    Waterson offered up a prayer,
Then the coffin was lowered into the grave by the pall-
    bearers there ;
'Twas then the friends began to cry for their sorrow was
    profound,
Then along with the people assembled there they left the
    burying-ground.

THE DEATH OF CAPTAIN WARD

'Twas about the beginning of the past century
Billy Bowls was pressed into the British Navy,
And conveyed on board the " Waterwitch " without delay,
Scarce getting time to bid farewell to the villagers of Fairway.

And once on board the " Waterwitch " he resolved to do his
duty,
And if he returned safe home he'd marry Nelly Blyth, his
beauty ;
And he'd fight for old England like a jolly British tar,
And the thought of Nelly Blyth would solace him during
the war.

Poor fellow, he little thought what he had to go through,
But in all his trials at sea he never did rue ;
No, the brave tar became reconciled to his fate,
And felt proud of his commander, Captain Ward the Great.

And on board the " Waterwitch " was Tom Riggles, his old
comrade,
And with such a comrade he seldom felt afraid ;
Because the stories they told each other made the time pass
quickly away,
And made their hearts feel light and gay.

'Twas on a Sunday morning and clear to the view,
Captain Ward the attention of his men he drew ;
" Look! " he cried, " There's two French men-of-war on
our right,
Therefore prepare, my lads, immediately to begin the fight."

Then the " Waterwitch " was steered to the ship that was
most near,
While every man resolved to sell their lives most dear ;
But the French commander disinclined to engage in the
fight,
And he ordered his men to put on a press of canvas and
take to flight.

Then Captain Ward gave the order to fire,
Then Billy Bowls cried, " Now we'll get fighting to our
hearts' desire " ;
And for an hour a running fight was maintained,
And the two ships of the enemy near upon the "Waterwitch"
gained.

Captain Ward walked the deck with a firm tread,
When a shot from the enemy pierced the ship, yet he felt no
dread ;
But with a splinter Bill Bowls was wounded on the left arm,
And he cried, " Death to the frog-eaters, they have done me
little harm."

Then Captain Ward cried, " Fear not, my men, we will win
the day,
Now, men, pour in a broadside without delay " ;
Then they sailed around the " St. Denis " and the " Gloire,"
And in their cabin windows they poured a deadly fire.

The effect on the two ships was tremendous to behold,
But the Frenchmen stuck to their guns with courage
bold ;
And the crash and din of artillery was deafening to the ear,
And the cries of the wounded men were pitiful to hear.

Then Captain Ward to his men did say,
" We must board the Frenchman without delay " ;
Then he seized his cutlass as he spoke,
And jumped on board the " St. Denis " in the midst of the
smoke.

Then Bill Bowls and Tom Riggles hastily followed him,
Then, hand to hand, the battle did begin ;
And the men sprang upon their foe and beat them back,
And hauled down their colours and hoisted the Union
Jack.

But the men on board the " St. Denis " fought desperately
hard,
And just as the " St. Denis " was captured a ball struck
Captain Ward
Right on the forehead, and he fell without a groan,
And for the death of Captain Ward the men did moan.

Then the first lieutenant who was standing near by,
Loudly to the men did cry,
" Come, men, and carry your noble commander below ;
But there's one consolation, we have beaten the foe."

And thus fell Captain Ward in the prime of life,
But I hope he is now in the better world free from strife;
But, alas! 'tis sad to think he was buried in the mighty
deep,
Where too many of our brave seamen silently sleep.

Oh! God, I thank Thee for restoring King Edward the
    Seventh's health again,
And let all his subjects throughout the Empire say Amen ;
May God guard him by night and day,
At home and abroad, when he's far away.

May angels guard his bed at night when he lies down,
And may his subjects revere him, and on him do not frown ;
May he be honoured by them at home and abroad,
And may he always be protected by the Eternal God.

My blessing on his noble form, and on his lofty head,
May all good angels guard him while living and when dead ;
And when the final hour shall come to summons him away,
May his soul be wafted to the realms of bliss I do pray.

Long may he reign, happy and serene,
Also his Queen most beautiful to be seen ;
And may God guard his family by night and day,
That they may tread in the paths of virtue and not go astray.

May God prosper King Edward the Seventh wherever he
    goes,
May he always reign victorious over his foes ;
Long may he be spared to wear the British Crown,
And may God be as a hedge around him at night when he
    lies down ;
May God inspire him with wisdom, and long may he reign
As Emperor of India and King Edward the VII.—Amen.

A SOLDIER'S REPRIEVE

'Twas in the United States of America some years ago
An aged father sat at his fireside with his heart full of woe,
And talking to his neighbour, Mr Allan, about his boy
    Bennie
That was to be shot because found asleep doing sentinel duty.

" Inside of twenty-four hours, the telegram said,
And, oh! Mr Allan, he's dead, I am afraid.
Where is my brave Bennie now to me is a mystery."
" We will hope with his heavenly Father," said Mr Allan,
    soothingly.

" Yes, let us hope God is very merciful," said Mr Allan.
" Yes, yes," said Bennie's father, " my Bennie was a good
    man.
He said, ' Father, I'll go and fight for my country.'
' Go, then, Bennie,' I said, ' and God be with ye.' "

Little Blossom, Bennie's sister, sat listening with a blanched
    cheek,
Poor soul, but she didn't speak,
Until a gentle tap was heard at the kitchen door,
Then she arose quickly and tripped across the floor.

And opening the door, she received a letter from a neigh-
    bour's hand,
And as she looked upon it in amazement she did stand.
Then she cried aloud, " It is from my brother Bennie.
Yes, it is, dear father, as you can see."

And as his father gazed upon it he thought Bennie was dead,
Then he handed the letter to Mr Allan and by him it was read,
And the minister read as follows : " Dear father, when this
  you see
I shall be dead and in eternity.

" And, dear father, at first it seemed awful to me
The thought of being launched into eternity.
But, dear father, I'm resolved to die like a man,
And keep up my courage and do the best I can.

" You know I promised Jemmie Carr's mother to look after
  her boy,
Who was his mother's pet and only joy.
But one night while on march Jemmie turned sick,
And if I hadn't lent him my arm he'd have dropped very
  quick.

" And that night it was Jemmie's turn to be sentry,
And take poor Jemmie's place I did agree,
But I couldn't keep awake, father, I'm sorry to relate,
And I didn't know it, well, until it was too late.

"Good-bye, dear father, God seems near me,
But I'm not afraid now to be launched into eternity.
No, dear father, I'm going to a world free from strife,
And see my Saviour there in a better, better life."

That night, softly, little Blossom, Bennie's sister, stole out
And glided down the footpath without any doubt.
She was on her way to Washington, with her heart full of
  woe,
To try and save her brother's life, blow high, blow low.

And when Blossom appeared before President Lincoln,
Poor child, she was looking very woebegone.
Then the President said, " My child, what do you want with
   me ? "
"Please, Bennie's life, sir," she answered timidly.

" Jemmie was sick, sir, and my brother took his place."
" What is this you say, child ? Come here and let me see
   your face."
Then she handed him Bennie's letter, and he read it care-
   fully,
And taking up his pen he wrote a few lines hastily.

Then he said to Blossom, " To-morrow, Bennie will go with
   you."
And two days after this interview
Bennie and Blossom took their way to their green mountain
   home,
And poor little Blossom was footsore, but she didn't moan.

And a crowd gathered at the mill depot to welcome them
   back,
And to grasp the hand of his boy, Farmer Owen wasn't
   slack,
And tears flowed down his cheeks as he said fervently,
" The Lord be praised for setting my dear boy free."

RICHARD PIGOTT, THE FORGER

Richard Pigott, the forger, was a very bad man,
And to gainsay it there's nobody can,
Because for fifty years he pursued a career of deceit,
And as a forger few men with him could compete.

For by forged letters he tried to accuse Parnell
For the Phoenix Park murders, but mark what befel.
When his conscience smote him he confessed to the fraud,
And the thought thereof no doubt drove him mad.

Then he fled from London without delay,
Knowing he wouldn't be safe there night nor day,
And embarked on board a ship bound for Spain,
Thinking he would escape detection there, but 'twas all in
vain.

Because while staying at a hotel in Spain
He appeared to the landlord to be a little insane.
And he noticed he was always seemingly in dread,
Like a person that had committed a murder and afterwards
fled.

And when arrested in the hotel he seemed very cool,
Just like an innocent schoolboy going to school.
And he said to the detectives, " Wait until my portmanteau
I've got."
And while going for his portmanteau, himself he shot.

So perished Richard Pigott, a forger bold,
Who tried to swear Parnell's life away for the sake of gold,
But the vengeance of God overtook him,
And Parnell's life has been saved, which I consider no sin.

Because he was a man that was very fond of gold,
Not altogether of the miser's craving, I've been told,
But a craving desire after good meat and drink,
And to obtain good things by foul means he never did shrink.

He could eat and drink more than two ordinary men,
And to keep up his high living by foul means we must him
  condemn,
Because his heart's desire in life was to fare well,
And to keep up his good living he tried to betray Parnell.

Yes, the villain tried hard to swear his life away,
But God protected him by night and by day,
And during his long trial in London, without dismay,
The noble patriot never flinched nor tried to run away.

Richard Pigott was a man that was blinded by his own
  conceit.
And would have robbed his dearest friend all for good meat,
To satisfy his gluttony and his own sensual indulgence,
Which the inhuman monster considered no great offence.

But now in that undiscovered country he's getting his
  reward,
And I'm sure few people have for him little regard,
Because he was a villain of the deepest dye,
And but few people for him will heave a sigh.

When I think of such a monster my blood runs cold,
He was like Monteith, that betrayed Wallace for English
  gold ;
But I hope Parnell will prosper for many a day
In despite of his enemies that tried to swear his life away.

Oh! think of his sufferings and how manfully he did stand.
During his long trial in London, to me it seems grand.
To see him standing at the bar, innocent and upright,
Quite cool and defiant, a most beautiful sight.

And to the noble patriot, honour be it said,
He never was the least afraid
To speak on behalf of Home Rule for Ireland,
But like a true patriot nobly he did take his stand.

And may he go on conquering and conquer to the end,
And hoping that God will the right defend,
And protect him always by night and by day,
At home and abroad when far away.

And now since he's set free, Ireland's sons should rejoice
And applaud him to the skies, all with one voice,
For he's their patriot, true and bold,
And an honest, true-hearted gentleman be it told.

THE TROUBLES OF MATTHEW MAHONEY

In a little town in Devonshire, in the mellow September
    moonlight,
A gentleman passing along a street saw a pitiful sight,
A man bending over the form of a woman on the pavement.
He was uttering plaintive words and seemingly discontent.

" What's the matter with the woman ? " asked the gentle-
    man,
As the poor, fallen woman he did narrowly scan.
" There's something the matter, as yer honour can see,
But it's not right to prate about my wife, blame me."

" Is that really your wife ? " said the gentleman.
" Yes, sor, but she looks very pale and wan."
" But surely she is much younger than you ? "
" Only fourteen years, sor, that is thrue.

" It's myself that looks a deal oulder nor I really am,
Throuble have whitened my hair, my good gintleman,
Which was once as black as the wings of a crow,
And it's throuble as is dyed it as white as the snow.

Come, my dear sowl, Bridget, it's past nine o'clock,
And to see yez lying there it gives my heart a shock."
And he smoothed away the raven hair from her forehead,
And her hands hung heavily as if she had been dead.

The gentleman saw what was the matter and he sighed
    again,
And he said, " It's a great trial and must give you pain,
But I see you are willing to help her all you can."
But the encouraging words was not lost upon the Irishman.

" Thrial! " he echoed, " Don't mintion it, yer honour,
But the blessing of God rest upon her.
Poor crathur, she's good barrin' this one fault,
And by any one I don't like to hear her miscault."

" What was the reason of her taking to drink ? "
" Bless yer honour, that's jest what I oftentimes think,
Some things is done without any rason at all,
And, sure, this one to me is a great downfall.

' Ah, Bridget, my darlin', I never dreamt ye'd come to
   this,"
And stooping down, her cheek he did kiss.
While a glittering tear flashed in the moonlight to the ground,
For the poor husband's grief was really profound.

" Have you any children ? " asked the gentleman.
" No, yer honour, bless the Lord, contented I am,
I wouldn't have the lambs know any harm o' their mother,
Besides, sor, to me they would be a great bother."

" What is your trade, my good man ? "
" Gardening, sor, and mighty fond of it I am.
Kind sor, I am out of a job and I am dying with sorrow."
" Well, you can call at my house by ten o'clock to-morrow.

" And I'll see what I can do for you.
Now, hasten home with your wife, and I bid you adieu.
But stay, my good man, I did not ask your name."
" My name is Matthew Mahoney, after Father Matthew of
   great fame."

Then Mahoney stooped and lifted Bridget tenderly,
And carried her home in his arms cheerfully,
And put her to bed while he felt quite content,
Still hoping Bridget would see the folly of drinking and
   repent.

And at ten o'clock next morning Matthew was at Blandford
   Hall,
And politely for Mr Gillespie he did call,
But he was told Mrs Gillespie he would see,
And was invited into the parlour cheerfully.

And when Mrs Gillespie entered the room
She said, " Matthew Mahoney, I suppose you want to know your doom.
Well, Matthew, tell your wife to call here to-morrow."
" I'll ax her, my lady, for my heart's full of sorrow."

So Matthew got his wife to make her appearance at Blandford Hall,
And, trembling, upon Mrs Gillespie poor Bridget did call,
And had a pleasant interview with Mrs Gillespie,
And was told she was wanted for a new lodge-keeper immediately.

" But, Bridget, my dear woman, you musn't drink any more,
For you have got a good husband you ought to adore,
And Mr Gillespie will help you, I'm sure,
Because he is very kind to deserving poor."

And Bridget's repentance was hearty and sincere,
And by the grace of God she never drank whisky, rum, or beer,
And good thoughts come into her mind of Heaven above,
And Matthew Mahoney dearly does her love.

DAVID WINTER AND SON LTD., PRINTERS, DUNDEE